FROM REMARKABLE HITTING FEATS TO INTEGRATION AND A WAR THAT SENT BIG LEAGUERS ABROAD, THESE ARE THE PLAYERS AND STORIES THAT DEFINED THE 1940s.

DECADES

1940–1949

Baseball Insiders Library®

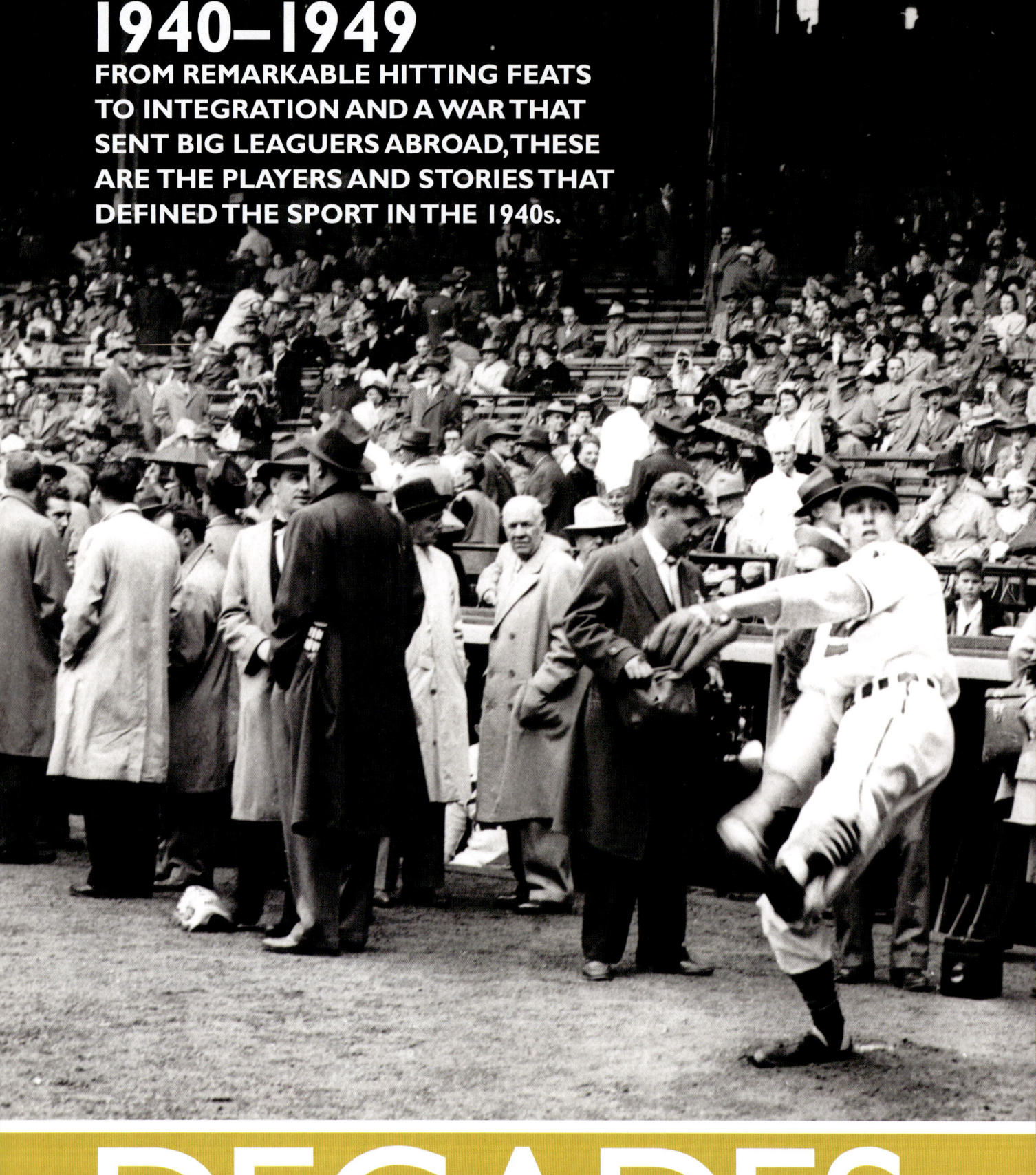

1940–1949

FROM REMARKABLE HITTING FEATS TO INTEGRATION AND A WAR THAT SENT BIG LEAGUERS ABROAD, THESE ARE THE PLAYERS AND STORIES THAT DEFINED THE SPORT IN THE 1940s.

DECADES

DECADES: 1940–1949 by Jerry Crasnick

From remarkable hitting feats to integration and a war that sent Big Leaguers abroad, these are the players and stories that defined the sport in the 1940s.

Printed in 2011

ABOUT THE AUTHOR

Jerry Crasnick has covered Major League Baseball for more than two decades. He has written for ESPN.com *since 2003, after previously working for the* Cincinnati Post, Denver Post *and* Bloomberg News. *He has authored* License to Deal: A Season on the Run With a Maverick Baseball Agent *as well as* Decades: 2000–2009, Decades: 1950–1959 *and* Decades: 1980–1989 *in the* Baseball Insiders Library®. *He lives with his wife and two daughters in Langhorne, Pa.*

ACKNOWLEDGEMENTS

Major League Baseball would like to thank Pat Kelly and Milo Stewart Jr. at the National Baseball Hall of Fame and Museum for their invaluable assistance; as well as Eric Enders and David Crawford Jones for their diligent work in helping to prepare this book for publication.

MAJOR LEAGUE BASEBALL PROPERTIES

Vice President, Publishing
Donald S. Hintze

Editorial Director
Mike McCormick

Publications Art Director
Faith M. Rittenberg

Senior Production Manager
Claire Walsh

Managing Editor
Jon Schwartz

Senior Publishing Coordinator
Anamika Panchoo

Associate Art Director
Mark Calimbas

Project Editor
Jake Schwartzstein

Project Assistant Editors
Allison Duffy, Paul Boye

Editorial Interns
Nicholas Carroll, Bill San Antonio

MAJOR LEAGUE BASEBALL PHOTOS

Director
Rich Pilling

Photo Editor
Jessica Foster

MLB INSIDERS CLUB

Managing Editor
Jen Weaverling

Art Director
Brian Peterson

Proofreader
Travis Bullinger

1 2 3 4 5 6 7 8 9 10 / 12 11

© MLB Insiders Club 2011

ISBN: 978-1-58159-539-0

All rights reserved. No part of this publication may be reproduced, stored in an electronic retrieval system or transmitted in any form or by any means (electronic, photocopying, recording or otherwise) without the prior or written permission of the copyright owner.

MLB Insiders Club
12301 Whitewater Drive
Minnetonka, MN 55343

TABLE OF CONTENTS

Introduction	6
Chapter 1: Hitting Feats	8
Chapter 2: Pitching Feats	24
Chapter 3: The Changing Game	34
Chapter 4: Baseball During Wartime	44
Chapter 5: In the Front Office	60
Chapter 6: Integration	70
Chapter 7: Amazing Rookie Seasons	86
Chapter 8: Sacrifice	102
Chapter 9: Characters and Controversy	110
Chapter 10: Pennant Races	128
Chapter 11: World Series	136
Chapter 12: Emotional Moments	146
Source Notes/Credits	156
Index	159

INTRODUCTION

Baseball fans were treated to some amazing displays of artistry and skill during the 1940s. How could the quality of play not be special when legends like Joe DiMaggio, Ted Williams and Stan Musial were in the prime of their careers, and Bob Feller threw his fastball with enough zip to outpace a Harley-Davidson in full throttle?

After DiMaggio hit safely in 56 straight games in 1941, generations of hitters took their best shot at replicating the feat and failed to come close. Same goes for hitting .400 in a season, a mark that Williams passed when he hit .406, also in 1941.

Feller was so imposing as a young fireballer with Cleveland that Major League Baseball arranged for a "competition" at Chicago's Lincoln Park in 1940. Feller's fastball beat a speeding motorcycle to a designated target by several feet. When the velocity of Feller's heater was estimated at 104 mph, the nickname "Rapid Robert" took on a whole new meaning.

Baseball history books also herald Detroit pitcher Hal Newhouser's two MVP Awards during the war years, Enos Slaughter's 270-foot sprint to glory in the 1946 World Series, Mel Ott's 500th career homer and Lefty Grove's 300th win. But when the final accounting was done, milestones and championship celebrations paled in comparison to the off-the-field developments. Baseball in the 1940s was notable for upheaval and widespread change, forged against a backdrop of heartache and hard choices.

From the moment Japan attacked the U.S. naval base at Pearl Harbor, Hawaii, in December 1941, baseball became part of the tableau. Star ballplayers left their families and professional aspirations behind to help fight the Axis menace in World War II. Some never came home, and many who did return were never quite the same.

The departure of so many established Major Leaguers created a chance for those who might not otherwise have received it. A 15-year-old pitcher named Joe Nuxhall woke up one day standing on the Cincinnati Reds' Crosley Field mound, 60 feet, six inches away from the great Musial. With just one arm, Pete Gray played outfield with the St. Louis Browns, and fans who needed a baseball fix with no thought to the gender of the players flocked to see the Rockford Peaches in the All-American Girls Professional Baseball League.

Just when the war ended and the game was settling back into its comfortable old rhythms, Dodgers General Manager Branch Rickey changed the world. He summoned a young Negro Leagues infielder named Jackie Robinson to his Brooklyn office in August 1945, and they formed a partnership that would alter the face of both baseball and society.

Robinson played his first game with the Dodgers in 1947, and the impact was both immediate and profound. For millions of African-American youths, Robinson was more than an inspiration; he was opportunity personified. That was true for kids playing stickball on asphalt schoolyards in Brooklyn, and a talented youngster named Henry Aaron in Alabama.

"You have to remember that in those days, there weren't many things black people could do," Aaron said. "You could teach, or be a fighter or maybe a singer. Before Jackie, I took it for granted that the only professional baseball I could play would be in the Negro Leagues. I had no idea I could play in the Majors because there were no doors open at the time."

Jackie kicked open the door, and generations of aspiring ballplayers were happy to follow.

In a time of war and uncertainty, baseball persevered. These are the stories of the men and women who carried the game, who etched their names in the granite of baseball lore, forever immortalized in the decade that bore them all: the 1940s.

The charismatic Satchel Paige shined in the Negro Leagues for years before doing the same in the Majors following the sport's integration in 1947.

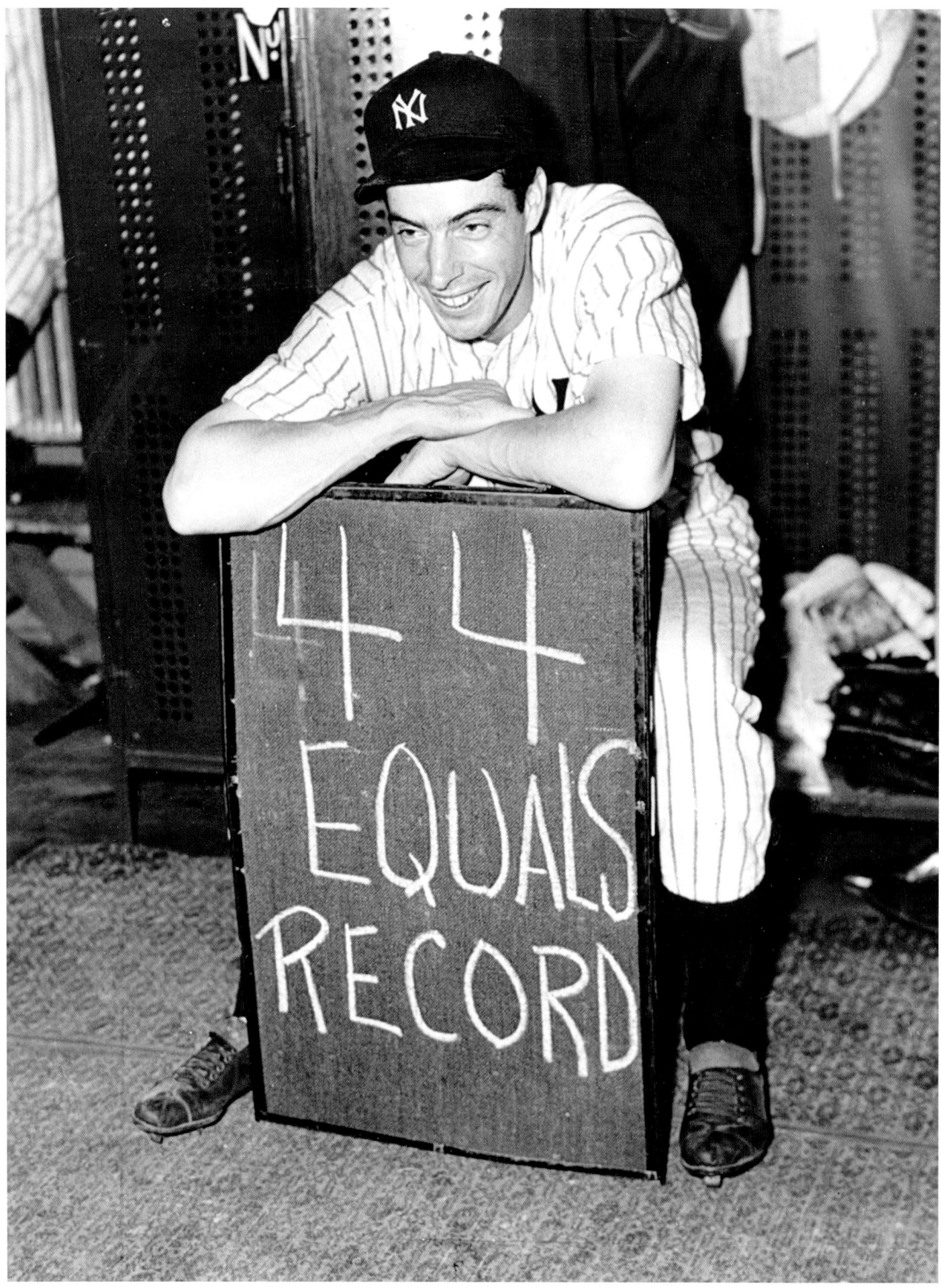

CHAPTER I
HITTING FEATS

What are the odds that two once-in-a-lifetime hitting achievements would unfold over the span of a single season? The Boston Red Sox's Ted Williams demoralized American League pitchers on the way to batting .406 in 1941, yet Teddy Ballgame failed to receive the Most Valuable Player Award for his efforts. That honor went to Yankees center fielder Joe DiMaggio, who rapped out a seemingly innocuous single in a 13-1 loss to the Chicago White Sox on May 15 and didn't pause for a breath until after the All-Star Game. Two months after that single, DiMaggio and the number "56" would be linked for eternity.

GOING STREAKING

JOE DIMAGGIO'S IMAGE as a larger-than-life baseball figure was both a product of his athletic skill and his regal demeanor on and off the diamond. He tracked down balls in center field with grace, wore stylish suits, married Hollywood starlet Marilyn Monroe and attracted legions of admirers as the embodiment of cool.

From his heyday in the 1940s to his post-career incarnation as Mr. Coffee spokesman and "Baseball's Greatest Living Ballplayer," DiMaggio would be immortalized for decades in song and popular culture as the venerated "Yankee Clipper."

"Baseball isn't statistics," columnist Jimmy Breslin once observed. "It's Joe DiMaggio rounding second base."

Still, no game reveres its statistical achievements more than baseball. And in the final accounting, DiMaggio's signature milestone is one that baseball experts think might be the most difficult to surpass.

DIMAGGIO DURING THE STREAK

G	AVG	R	2B	3B	HR	RBI	SLG
56	.408	56	16	4	15	55	.717

DiMaggio was hitting a pedestrian (for him) .306 when he singled in New York's 13-1 loss to Eddie Smith and the Chicago White Sox on May 15, 1941. He banged out two hits the next day, went 1 for 3 the day after that, and built an inexorable momentum until his streak became a national obsession.

Before DiMaggio was through, he had hit safely in 56 straight games — obliterating the previous mark of 45 set by Wee Willie Keeler of the Baltimore Orioles in 1896–97 (Keeler's single-season record stood at 44).

DiMaggio poses after tying Keeler's single-season record of 44 consecutive games with a hit; he would shatter the mark by getting base knocks in 12 more games.

DiMaggio's streak ended on July 17 against Cleveland, thanks in large part to some sterling defensive plays by Indians third baseman Ken Keltner. Incredibly, DiMaggio would reel off another 16-game streak before his next oh-fer — making it 72 out of 73 games with at least one hit. Decades later, as historians paid tribute to DiMaggio's hand-eye coordination and composure under fire, "The Streak" had taken on a mythology of its own as one of the game's most revered and unapproachable feats.

THE LAST TRAIN TO .400

TED WILLIAMS FAMOUSLY observed that his main goal upon retiring from Major League Baseball was to walk down the street one day and have onlookers declare, "There goes the greatest hitter that ever lived." Williams' 521 career home runs, .344 average and six batting titles are an eloquent testament to his skill, but if historians, fans, journalists and opponents are looking for a definitive statement on his brilliance, they need look no further than the events of Sept. 28, 1941, at the Philadelphia Athletics' Shibe Park. The "Splendid Splinter" entered Boston's season-ending doubleheader against the A's with a batting average of .3995 — a figure that would have been rounded up to .400 had he been willing to stay glued to the bench. But it wasn't Williams' style to play spectator.

"I'll play," Williams told reporters. "Hitting .3995 ain't hitting .400. If I'm going to be a .400 hitter, I want more than my toenails on the line."

All Williams did in the doubleheader was hit safely six times in eight at-bats to finish at .406 and remove all doubt, as well as the need to round up. Although accomplished hitters from George Brett to Tony Gwynn made spirited runs at .400 in later years, Williams remains the last hitter to cross that lofty threshold. Williams' only shortcoming in 1941 was bad timing. He won the All-Star Game with a dramatic walk-off homer and proved his mettle on the final day against the A's, but he finished a close second in the American League MVP balloting to Joe DiMaggio — author of that storied 56-game hitting streak.

THE BRIGHTEST STAR

Despite his immense success, Ted Williams struggled to steal the national spotlight from Joe DiMaggio. While DiMaggio won nine World Series and played for the Major Leagues' premier team, Williams played on a Red Sox club in the midst of the Curse of the Bambino. Even in Williams' banner season in 1941, a year in which he hit .406, he was outshined by DiMaggio's 56-game hitting streak and finished second in the voting for American League MVP.

But the Splendid Splinter stole the show at the 1941 Midsummer Classic. After DiMaggio grounded to shortstop for the second out of the bottom of the ninth, Williams stepped up to the plate with the American League down a run and two men on base, placing the entire game squarely on his shoulders. Williams did not disappoint, slamming a high fly ball that just stayed fair down the right-field line for a three-run home run and a victory for the American League.

THE HAMMER'S APPRENTICE

HANK GREENBERG TOOK home two Most Valuable Player Awards and made four All-Star Games in a 13-year Hall-of-Fame career, all while building a reputation for sportsmanship, civility and class both on and off the field. Before retiring as a player in 1947, Greenberg passed along some friendship and wisdom that helped pave another budding slugger's way to stardom.

In January of '47, the Pittsburgh Pirates purchased the 36-year-old Greenberg's contract from the Detroit Tigers for $75,000, and "Hammerin' Hank" didn't take long to mesh with the team's young left fielder, Ralph Kiner. When Kiner was going through some struggles at the plate early in the season and the Pirates' front office was thinking about sending him back to the Minor Leagues, it was Greenberg who urged management to give his young teammate more time to prove himself.

Greenberg gave Kiner guidance on baseball and life. He invited Kiner to early batting practice and schooled his young protege on the fine art of crowding the plate and pulling pitches to left field. Away from the park, he gave Kiner tips on the proper way to dress. "He took me under his wing and became my mentor," Kiner said.

The Pirates moved the left-field fence in at Forbes Field and dubbed the space between the old wall and the new wall "Greenberg Gardens," but Kiner was the prime beneficiary. He hit 51 home runs in 1947 to tie the New York

Williams was all smiles during the 1941 campaign, when he became the 20th century's last Major Leaguer to finish a season with a .400 batting average.

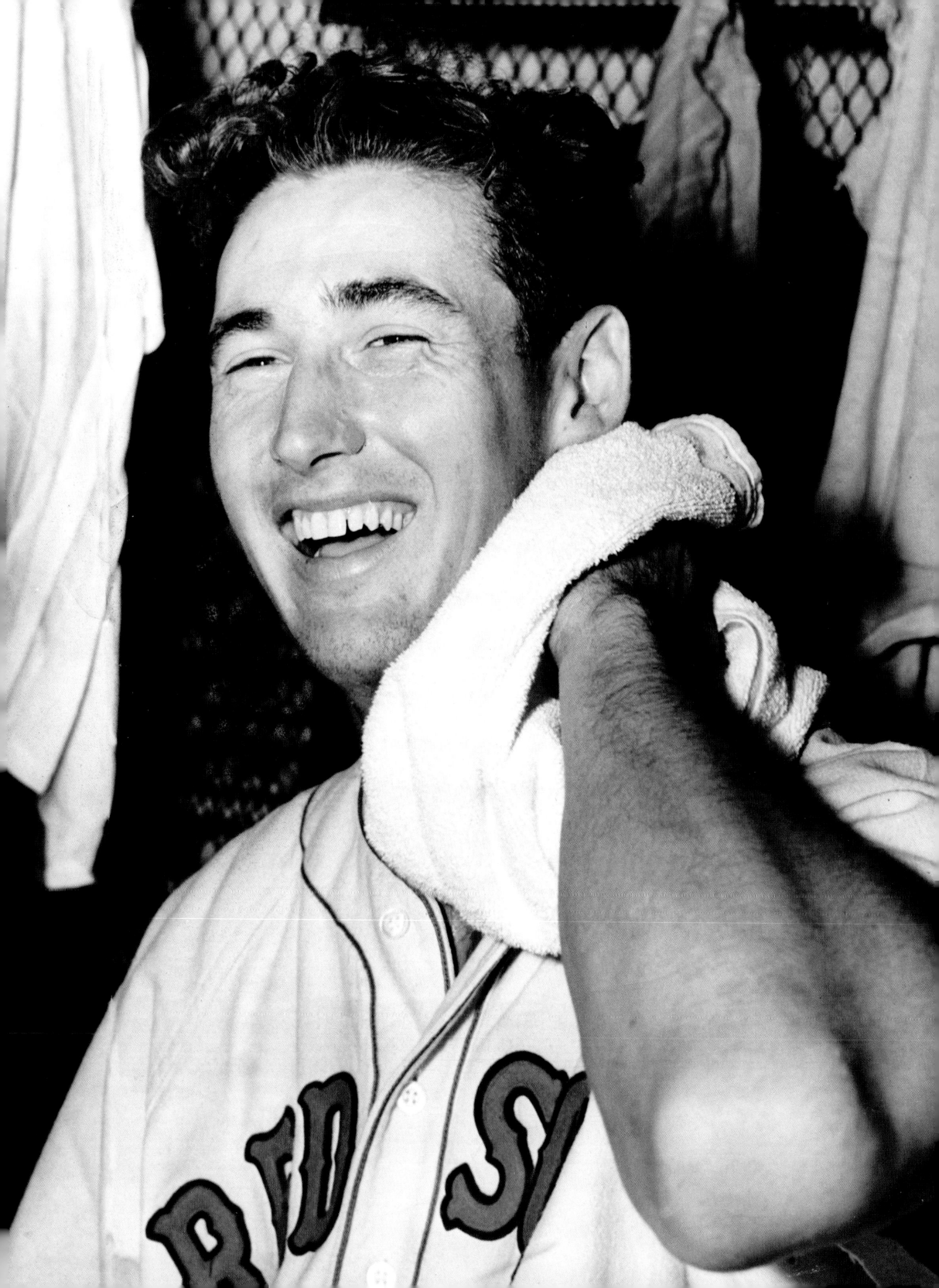

Giants' Johnny Mize for the National League lead. A year later, after Greenberg's retirement, the area was renamed "Kiner's Korner."

Greenberg and Kiner developed a mutual respect and a lifetime bond from their year together in Pittsburgh, and both sluggers eventually received their due with election to Cooperstown. When Greenberg died in 1986, Kiner, then a broadcaster with the New York Mets, called it "the saddest news I could possibly have heard."

THE 500 CLUB

MEL OTT WAS 18 years old when he hit his first Big League home run. He lined a ball to center field off Cubs pitcher Hal Carlson, and was the beneficiary of a major gift when Hack Wilson tried and failed to make a shoestring catch. The ball rolled away, and Ott circled the bases on an inside-the-parker for his only homer of the 1927 season.

The home run was memorably bizarre, but it was no fluke.

Ott went on to play 22 seasons in the Big Leagues with the New York Giants, and he made history in 1945 by joining Babe Ruth and Jimmie Foxx as the third in the 500–home run club. Ott's milestone shot came off Boston's Johnny Hutchings in a 9-2 Giants victory over the Braves at the Polo Grounds.

Ott, universally regarded as one of baseball's nicest, most admired players, had a premonition before the game that he would go deep. He shared that sentiment during the ride to the park with pitcher Carl Hubbell and Giants President Horace Stoneham.

"Mel asked Horace if he was ready to party after the game and Horace wanted to know why. Then it dawned on me. The sucker was going to hit his 500th homer," Hubbell said later.

Ott, dubbed "Master Melvin" upon his arrival in the Big Leagues because of his skill and youth, finished with 511 home runs. He was inducted into the Hall of Fame in 1951.

MUSCLES IN HIS MUSCLES

JIMMIE FOXX WASN'T especially huge, but his strength and ability to rattle the seats in distant regions of Major League parks prompted his contemporaries to refer to him as "The Beast." At 6 feet, 195 pounds, the man never met a fastball he couldn't punish.

"He was the only hitter I saw who could hit balls on his fist and still get them out of the park," said Hall-of-Fame pitcher Lefty Grove. "He has muscles in his muscles."

Foxx, who was also referred to as "Double X," carved out a reputation for himself as one of baseball's most feared sluggers during his heyday as a member of the Philadelphia A's and Boston Red Sox. His most significant achievement came on Sept. 24, 1940, when he went deep against Philadelphia's George Caster at Shibe Park to join Babe Ruth as the second player with 500 career home runs. "Babe Ruth could hit them far, but when Jimmie Foxx hit one, it was like a golf ball," said Cleveland pitcher Mel Harder. "He was the most powerful hitter I ever saw."

Foxx was elected to the Hall of Fame in 1951, but his life after baseball was marked by personal setbacks and tragedy. He battled drinking problems, made several ill-advised investments that forced him to declare bankruptcy, and died of a heart attack at age 59 after choking on a piece of meat while having dinner with his brother. But his reputation as one of baseball's best-liked stars and formidable hitters endured long after his passing.

MOST HOME RUNS BY AGE 30	
Alex Rodriguez	409
Ken Griffey Jr.	398
Jimmie Foxx	**379**
Mickey Mantle	374
Eddie Mathews	370
Albert Pujols	366
Andruw Jones	345
Hank Aaron	342
Mel Ott	342
Juan Gonzalez	340

The diminutive Ott was a monster with his bat, becoming the third player to reach 500 career home runs.

HITTING FEATS

At age 32, the burly Foxx became the youngest player to reach 500 career home runs and held that mark until 2007, when Alex Rodriguez broke it.

HITTING FEATS

DO-OVER

IN MOST CASES, reaching 3,000 career hits is obviously a once-in-a-lifetime thrill. Paul Waner's sense of integrity and fair play allowed him to experience the moment twice.

Waner, a four-time All-Star with the Pittsburgh Pirates — and the "Big Poison" half of a brotherly tandem with his younger sibling Lloyd — was in the latter stages of his career and playing outfield for the Boston Braves in 1942 when his big moment arrived. He was sitting one hit shy of 3,000, and teammate Tommy Holmes was standing on first base when Boston Manager Casey Stengel signaled for the hit-and-run.

Reds shortstop Eddie Joost raced to cover second base, but had to apply the brakes and change direction when Waner hit a grounder into the vacated hole. When Joost failed to make the play, the official scorer signaled "base hit," the crowd erupted in cheers, and umpire John "Beans" Reardon retrieved the ball in anticipation of giving Waner his souvenir.

But Waner declined to accept the gift single. He looked at official scorer Jerry Moore in the press box and waved off the hit. Moore obliged, giving Joost an error, and Waner had to wait two days to officially record No. 3,000. Waner, a notorious drinker, reportedly sent a note to reporters afterward that said, "Boys, let's have a party tonight."

"He had to be a very graceful player," Casey Stengel once said of Waner. "Because he could slide without breaking the bottle on his hip."

NO EASY OUT

BOSTON BRAVES FOURTH-YEAR outfielder Tommy Holmes established a modern-day National League record on the way to a career-best .352 batting average in the summer of 1945, recording a 37-game hitting streak that would stand for more than three decades as the Senior Circuit benchmark, until the Cincinnati Reds' Pete Rose connected in 44 consecutive contests during the 1978 campaign.

Far left: Waner wouldn't let a cheap hit stand as his 3,000th. Near left: Holmes displayed an unrivaled ability to make contact.

17

Incredibly, the streak was only the second most impressive statistical achievement for Holmes that year. In 713 plate appearances with the Braves, Holmes led the league with 28 home runs while striking out just nine times.

Holmes never came close to matching that production when World War II ended and the game's top pitchers returned from military service, but his popularity with Braves fans remained strong. He was known as a hard-working, blue-collar player who took pains to fulfill every autograph request. Upon Holmes' death in 2008, one member of the Boston Braves Historical Society observed, "Tommy Holmes is as beloved to Braves fans as Johnny Pesky is to Red Sox fans."

'JUNIOR'S' CIRCUIT

In November 1947, Boston Red Sox Owner Tom Yawkey sent six nondescript players and $310,000 to the St. Louis Browns for righty pitcher Jack Kramer and shortstop Vern Stephens. It didn't take long for Yawkey to receive a handsome return on his investment. Stephens, a three-time All-Star with the Browns and key figure in St. Louis's 1944 pennant run, raised his game to new heights as part of a star-studded lineup with Ted Williams, Bobby Doerr and Dom DiMaggio in Boston.

In 1949, Stephens set Major League records for shortstops with 39 home runs and 159 runs batted in, finishing in seventh place in the American League MVP race. Stephens, nicknamed "Junior," retired because of knee problems at age 35 and died of a heart attack at age 48. He fell short of induction into the Hall of Fame in a Veterans Committee vote in 2008, and his biggest supporters maintain that he has never received the recognition that he deserves.

AN EARLY WALLBANGER

Pete Reiser made a major impression with the Brooklyn Dodgers in 1941, leading the National League in runs, doubles, triples, slugging percentage and total bases while hitting .343 to capture the batting title at age 22. But Reiser quickly became a victim of his hyper-aggressive style of play and lack of discretion around outfield fences.

Reiser's most celebrated encounter with a wall came in 1942, when he put himself in the hospital chasing a fly ball off the bat of the Cardinals' Enos Slaughter. Before Reiser's career ended, he was carried off the field on a stretcher 11 times. He suffered several concussions and broken bones, and was once injured so severely that he reportedly received the last rites.

"Pete may have been born to be the best baseball player that ever lived, but there never was a park big enough to contain his effort," wrote the great columnist Red Smith. "He was a man of immeasurable skills and unconquerable spirit who played the only way he knew how — hitting, running, sliding, crashing into outfield walls — until he had literally broken his magnificent body to bits."

When Reiser retired in 1952, his final stats — 786 hits and a .295 batting average — didn't come close to matching his once boundless potential. "You ask me the best player in my time and I say, unquestionably, Willie Mays," said Hall-of-Fame manager Leo Durocher. "With the possible exception of Pete Reiser.'"

THE ART OF .400

When a 16-year-old wunderkind with blazing speed by the name of Willie Mays showed up to play outfield for the Birmingham Black Barons in the Negro Leagues

The only thing that could match Reiser's potential was his fearlessness, which ultimately led to his early retirement.

during the 1948 season, he received some welcome guidance from a 27-year-old veteran infielder and teammate.

"I owe a lot of debt to him," Mays said of Artie Wilson, a mentor whose quiet, friendly manner earned him the nickname "The Birmingham Gentleman." But civility wasn't Wilson's only legacy. The man could also hit.

In the summer of '48, Wilson hit .402 for the Barons to become the first professional player to bat .400 since Ted Williams achieved the feat with the Boston Red Sox in 1941. Wilson made his only Big League stint three years later, joining the New York Giants for 19 games before being sent back to the Oakland Oaks in the Pacific Coast League. His spot on the New York roster was taken, fittingly, by a budding star named Willie Mays.

TWO-TIME CHAMP

JOHN JORDAN "BUCK" O'Neil spent a lifetime in baseball spreading joy and making other people better. As a prominent Negro Leagues manager with the Kansas City Monarchs, he was widely acclaimed for sending Ernie Banks, Elston Howard, Satchel Paige, "Sweet Lou" Johnson and numerous others on to successful careers in the Major Leagues.

But the influence of the man players lovingly called "Skip" transcended his nurturing side. He won a Negro Leagues batting title with the Kansas City Monarchs in 1940 and picked up a second crown in 1946. Buck Leonard of the Homestead Grays later called O'Neil one of the finest ballplayers he had ever seen.

"I respected Buck in the clutch. He was that type of hitter," said Jimmie Crutchfield, a long-time outfielder with Birmingham, Indianapolis and Chicago in the Negro Leagues. "You had to pitch very carefully to him. A smart, highly intelligent ballplayer."

STARS AT SECOND

ONLY A HANDFUL of second basemen in Major League history have been good enough to earn enshrinement into the National Baseball Hall of Fame. Two of the most productive men ever to play the position were mainstays for marquee franchises throughout the 1940s. Joe Gordon, nicknamed "Flash" in reference to the comic book character, made nine All-Star teams as a New York Yankee and Cleveland Indian and hit 253 home runs during his career. He was an acrobatic defender, and is probably best remembered for taking home the 1942 American League MVP Award over Ted Williams, who won the Triple Crown that season. Bobby Doerr, dubbed the "Silent Captain of the Red Sox" by Williams for his stoic leadership and unassuming demeanor, was a remarkably consistent and reliable performer for 14 seasons in a Boston uniform. Doerr hit 15 or more home runs 10 times, and drove in 90 or more runs on eight occasions in an era when second basemen were known more as scrappy table-setters than run producers.

Doerr and Gordon had several things in common other than the position they manned on the diamond. They were both born in Southern California, had close ties to the state of Oregon and were also avid outdoorsmen who shared a strong passion for fishing. They also missed time because of military service in World War II, but the void in their resumes couldn't prevent their induction into Cooperstown. Doerr, Williams, Carl Yastrzemski and Jim Rice are the only Hall of Famers to have played their entire careers with the Red Sox organization. Gordon made it to Cooperstown through the Veterans Committee in 2009. The following year, *Wall Street Journal* writer Russell Adams wrote a piece ranking the all-time greatest Yankees, and rated Gordon as the ninth- best position player in franchise history.

Remembered most for his contributions to the game following his playing career, O'Neil could hit with the best of them in his day.

HITTING FEATS

Gordon (left) and Doerr hit far better than your typical second basemen, ranking among the best in the game during the 1940s.

CHAPTER 2
PITCHING FEATS

With Major League Baseball's pitching pool depleted by the clarion call to World War II, opportunities arose for journeymen, the velocity-impaired and a 15-year-old suburban Cincinnati schoolboy named Joe Nuxhall, who was sweating bullets when he took the mound at Crosley Field to face St. Louis Cardinals great Stan Musial. Bob Feller christened the decade with an Opening Day no-hitter in 1940, and Warren Span brought it to a close with a 21-win effort for the Boston Braves in 1949. Between those acknowledged masters, pitchers from Lefty Grove to Hal Newhouser to Satchel Paige all had their moments to savor.

OPENING DAY

CLEVELAND INDIANS PITCHER Bob Feller was a mere 21 years old at the beginning of the 1940 season, but he overwhelmed opposing lineups that year with an electric fastball, ultimately posting 27 wins against 11 losses with a 2.61 ERA in 320.1 innings pitched. Already in his fifth season, the precocious right-handed prodigy led the Junior Circuit in strikeouts, shutouts and complete games and finished second to the Detroit Tigers' Hank Greenberg in MVP balloting.

American League hitters couldn't say that Feller's season of dominance came without warning, as he announced his presence with authority in the season opener by holding the Chicago White Sox hitless in a 1-0 Cleveland victory. Feller's April gem remains the only Opening Day no-no in baseball history.

Feller's parents and his sister, Marguerite, were among 14,000 fans on hand at Comiskey Park in Chicago on a day that Feller later described as "cold, windy and Norway-gray." Feller had been shelled in his final Spring Training tune-up against the New York Giants, and it became evident early in his Opening Day start that he lacked control of his curveball. Forced to go exclusively with his fastball after the second frame, Feller would walk five batters during the game, but allow no hits.

Rapid Robert benefited from some stout defense as the zeroes kept accumulating on the scoreboard. Indians outfielder Ben Chapman made a fine running catch on the White Sox's Taft Wright in the fourth inning, and second baseman Ray Mack robbed pinch-hitter Larry Rosenthal of a hit in the eighth frame. Feller exercised discretion with two outs in the bottom of the ninth, walking pesky White Sox shortstop Luke Appling. Wright followed with a hard groundball to the right side, but Mack made a diving play for

Already a veteran ace at age 21, Feller tossed the only Opening Day no-hitter in Big League history in 1940.

the final out to seal the no-hitter. "I didn't have no-hit stuff that day," Feller would later say of that historic afternoon. "I've had much better stuff. But it was such a cold day, if you hit a ball on the fists, it was like you had a handful of bees stinging you." Feller went on to pitch two more no-hitters — in 1946 and 1951 — and twirled a remarkable 12 one-hitters during his Hall-of-Fame career.

LEGENDARY SHOWDOWN

IN FIVE ROLLICKING decades as a pitcher in both the Negro Leagues and the Major Leagues, as well as professional circuits in Mexico, Cuba and even the Dominican Republic, Satchel Paige had no peers when it came to bravado, imagination or the ability to entertain a crowd. During a famous 1942 encounter between his Pittsburgh Crawfords and the Homestead Grays, all of those inimitable attributes coalesced to provide some absolutely wonderful theater.

Paige's stature as a showman was enhanced by an oft-told tale of braggadocio from the 1942 Negro Leagues World Series. As legend has it, he intentionally walked the bases loaded in the eighth inning to face all-time great slugger Josh Gibson. When the pair had crossed paths while playing in Puerto Rico, Gibson had kiddingly promised to take Paige deep when they faced each other with the bags full. According to some accounts, Paige walked either one or two batters on purpose to load the bases before striking out Gibson, finishing him off with a slow sidearm curve.

"They had to halt play for about an hour to clear the baseball field of straw hats," Paige later recalled.

No surprise, but a thorough dissection of Paige's story showed that it might have been embellished. In Satchel: The Life and Times of an American Legend, author Larry Tye cited newspaper accounts that never mentioned Paige issuing a walk in the inning, "intentional or otherwise." And while Paige did strike out Gibson with the bases loaded, it happened in the seventh inning, not the eighth.

"What really happened? The sportswriters on the scene almost surely got it right," Tye wrote. "Satchel and his teammates probably saw the game with eyes ever more rose-tinted, which is how memory works with our grander accomplishments."

THE 'EEPHUS'

NECESSITY IS THE mother of invention, and few Major League pitchers embody that principle better than Pirates hurler Truett Banks "Rip" Sewell. A 17-game loser with Pittsburgh in 1941, Sewell suffered a potentially career-ending foot injury on Dec. 7 — the day the Japanese attacked Pearl Harbor — when he was accidentally shot in a hunting accident at home in his native Alabama.

Forced to alter his windup, Sewell began to tinker with a high, arching lob pitch that upset the timing of opposing hitters. He unveiled the blooper pitch in an exhibition game against the Detroit Tigers, and induced an awkward-looking strikeout from outfielder Dick Wakefield on a full count. Sewell's Pittsburgh teammate, outfielder Maurice Van Robays, christened the pitch the "eephus."

"Eephus ain't nothin', and that's a nothin' pitch," Van Robays said.

Armed with his new toy, Sewell posted back-to-back 21-win seasons for the Pirates in 1943 and '44, and experienced a moment to remember at the 1946 All-Star Game. With the American League leading, 9-0, NL skipper Charlie Grimm urged Sewell to throw the pitch to help energize the crowd at Fenway Park in Boston. Sewell tossed three straight

Regardless of whether the story behind his encounter with Gibson is true, Paige (left) was surely one of the sport's all-time greatest showmen.

bloopers to hometown favorite Ted Williams, who edged up to the front of the batter's box and deposited the final lob into the right-field bullpen.

"Yes, that was my first look at the eephus or oophus or whatever you call it," the "Splendid Splinter" later said.

RIP SEWELL'S EEPHUS ERA (1942–49)				
W-L	CG	SH	IP	K
103-65	100	15	1,455.1	412

While Williams was able to get a hold of Sewell's signature pitch, plenty other hitters continued to struggle with it. In the eight seasons after his devastating foot injury, Sewell pitched to a 103-65 record thanks largely to his inventive, idiosyncratic offering.

HOME-FRONT ACE

GROWING UP IN Detroit during the Great Depression, Hal Newhouser looked to his hometown baseball team to provide an escape from life's daily troubles. After hearing the radio broadcast of Goose Goslin driving in Mickey Cochrane with the winning run in

This page: Newhouser realized his dream, winning two MVP Awards with the Tigers. Next page: Sewell saved his career with the eephus pitch.

Detroit's 1935 World Series victory over the Chicago Cubs, he fantasized of some day donning a Tigers uniform.

After a standout high school career, Newhouser signed with the Tigers as an amateur free agent in 1939. He realized his dream that year at age 18 when he made his Major League debut pitching for the Tigers. Exempt from military service in World War II because of a leaky heart valve, Newhouser posted a combined 54-18 record as he won consecutive AL MVP Awards in 1944 and '45.

Known as "Prince Hal," Newhouser ascended to baseball royalty in Detroit during his MVP seasons, and twice led the league in K's. If he didn't receive his just due, it was because the talent pool had been diminished by the loss of so many players to the military. But Newhouser validated his awards with two more 20-win seasons in the late '40s.

"I know there were some people who looked down on some of his accomplishments because he pitched during the war," Hall of Famer George Kell said after Newhouser's death in 1998. "But he was a great pitcher before and after the war, too."

In 1997, Newhouser joined Charlie Gehringer, Hank Greenberg and Al Kaline as the only Tigers to have their uniform numbers retired (Ty Cobb, another former Tigers great, didn't have a uniform number).

NO. 300

ROBERT MOSES "LEFTY" Grove grew up as one of eight children in a coal mining family in Maryland but had no interest in spending his life in the mines. Instead, he found a natural outlet for his intensity — and ambition — on the ballfield.

As Grove developed the expansive array of pitches that would bring him success as a Big League pitcher, stories circulated of his hot temper and quick trigger. He allegedly bullied teammates and umpires alike, and responded to opposing hitters who had the temerity to bunt against him by sending them sprawling to the dirt.

"You never talked to him on the mound," former A's teammate Jimmy Dykes once said. "No matter if he was ahead by 10 or behind by one, he was plain fierce during a game."

Grove's tunnel vision served him well when his career was fading. At age 41, he reached one of baseball's most hallowed pitching milestones with a 10-6 win for the Boston Red Sox over Cleveland on July 25, 1941. With the victory, Grove became the seventh pitcher in the modern era to enter the 300-win club. He made it in his 451st career start, the second-fastest in history behind only Christy Mathewson.

"The thrill of a lifetime? This is it," Grove said after receiving the game ball from Boston teammate Dom DiMaggio. "Quit now? They'll have to cut the uniform off me."

Once the euphoria subsided, reality took hold. Grove informed Red Sox Owner Tom Yawkey that he was retiring on Dec. 7, 1941. That decision, though, was upstaged by much bigger news: The Japanese had attacked Pearl Harbor.

NO SWEAT

CHARLES "RED" BARRETT compiled a mediocre 69-69 record in 11 seasons in the Major Leagues. That type of statistical line typically gets a pitcher classified under the unflattering category of "nondescript." But Barrett stood above the crowd in one facet of the game: He was the Cy Young of pitching economy.

Barrett went 9-16 with a 4.06 ERA for the Boston Braves in 1944, but he was a master at sending the fans home in time for dinner. His most impressive performance came on Aug. 10, when he threw a complete-game two-hitter to beat the Cincinnati Reds, 2-0.

Grove was the second-fastest pitcher to win 300 games.

Barrett dispatched with the Reds in an astonishing 58 pitches, breaking the complete-game record of 65 pitches set by Cincinnati's Slim Sallee in 1919. He didn't walk or strike out a single batter.

Barrett was known in baseball circles for being carefree and extremely self-confident. He took part in jitterbugging contests, was on a first-name basis with Tommy Dorsey and other big bandleaders, and enjoyed getting up on stage and crooning with the boys. The Sporting News once referred to him as "the amiable thrush."

Because most fielders enjoy working behind quick pitchers, Barrett won points with his teammates for his no-frills approach. He had barely received the ball from the catcher when he was ready to throw his next pitch.

"I'm no strike-outer," Barrett said in a 1938 interview. "These strikeout pitchers are chumps in my book. Me, I try to make them hit that first ball. After all, those other guys out there are supposed to work, too. If everybody in business was like me there wouldn't be so many people out of jobs."

> "I'M NO STRIKE-OUTER. STRIKEOUT PITCHERS ARE CHUMPS. THOSE OTHER GUYS OUT THERE ARE SUPPOSED TO WORK, TOO." — RED BARRETT

BULLPEN POWER

SEVERAL DECADES BEFORE bullpen specialization was a key part of every game and high-profile closers began making enormous salaries and entering games to the accompaniment of their own personal theme music, the bullpen was viewed as the last outpost for middling pitchers who weren't good enough to crack starting rotations. Nevertheless, several relievers became known as difference makers during the 1940s.

Johnny Murphy, a right-hander from the Bronx, appeared in six World Series with the Yankees and went 12-4 with a 2.51 ERA in 1943. Murphy went by the nickname "Grandma," a reference either to his rocking pitching motion or tendency to complain about meals and accommodations on the road. He was partial to French wines and haute cuisine and often didn't find the typical ballplayer fare up to his standards.

Hilton Smith posted a 93-11 record between 1939 and 1942 as a starter with Kansas City in the Negro Leagues. Later in his career, he formed a dynamic 1-2 punch with Satchel Paige.

"Most people never heard of me," Smith said. "That's because I was Satchel Paige's relief. He'd go two or three innings, I'd go in there and save it. The next day I'd look in the paper and the headline would say, 'Satchel and Monarchs Win Again.'"

The general profile of relievers took a big step forward in 1947 thanks to dominant performances by the Dodgers' Hugh Casey and the Yankees' Joe Page. Casey developed into the NL's premier late-inning fireman after returning from naval service in WWII. And when Page was at his peak, his reputation preceded him as he entered a game in the late innings.

"It was like thunder, rolling, and it made a cave of the vast Stadium," wrote sportwriter W.C. Heinz. "They rose as one, all their shouts and screams one great roar, and the gate of the fence would open, and he would come out, immaculate in those pinstripes, walking with that sort of slow, shuffling gait, his warm-up jacket over his shoulder, a man on his way to work."

Barrett preferred to pitch to contact than go for the strikeout, and it helped him set a record for fewest pitches thrown in a complete game.

CHAPTER 3
THE CHANGING GAME

Sometimes change is just as meaningful when it takes place on the ground floor. A Pennsylvania lumberyard clerk named Carl Stotz had a brainstorm one day that it might be fun for kids to play baseball with uniforms on regulation fields, and he set his idea in motion. In 1947, the first Little League World Series took place in Williamsport, Pa. That same year, first baseman and eventual president of the United States George "Poppy" Bush led Yale to a spot in the first College World Series in Kalamazoo, Mich., against the University of California. Interest in both events continued to grow over the years, and the Little League and college showcases gave generations of players an opportunity to chase their dreams.

THE $100,000 MAN

NEW YORK YANKEES Owners Dan Topping and Del Webb were intent on making a statement with their wallets in the spring of 1949, when they planned to make star center fielder Joe DiMaggio the highest-paid player in the game. Babe Ruth had initially set the standard at $80,000 per year, and Cleveland ace Bob Feller surpassed him at $85,000, so Topping and Webb decided to go all-in and bump DiMaggio to $90,000 with a bonus based on the team's attendance.

That's when Bernard "Toots" Shor, the acclaimed New York tavern owner and DiMaggio confidant, decided to inject his two cents' worth.

"Del," Shor reportedly told Webb. "Ain't it worth another $10,000 to get your picture in all the papers with baseball's first $100,000 player?"

Topping and Webb agreed, and made DiMaggio the first six-figure-salaried player in baseball history. But all the publicity in the five boroughs couldn't resurrect the "Yankee Clipper" of old. DiMaggio was already 34 years old in 1949, and was troubled by numerous ailments and coming off surgery to repair a bone spur in his right heel.

"When he wasn't on the field, he could barely walk," author Richard Ben Cramer recalled in his book *Joe DiMaggio: The Hero's Life*. "Special shoes with high arches couldn't stop the stabbing. He was on painkillers all the time — and he was exhausted."

The Yankees continued to pay DiMaggio $100,000 for the rest of his playing career, but he was a shadow of his former self. After hitting .263 in 116 games in 1951, he surrendered to time and his fading skills, retiring at age 36.

DiMaggio was all smiles after becoming the first Big Leaguer ever to ink a $100,000 contract.

THE CHANGING GAME

THE CLOTHES MAKE THE MAN

THE CHICAGO CUBS may have lost four times in the World Series in a 10-year span from 1929–38, but they made a fashion statement on the field during the war years. In 1940, the Cubs became the first Major League team to wear sleeveless uniforms, only to abandon the look three years later upon finishing 38 games out of first place in the National League. The Cincinnati Reds later embraced the sleeveless look during the 1950s, and first baseman Ted Kluszewski modified it by eschewing the T-shirt underneath to help accomodate his muscular frame.

The Brooklyn Dodgers made a statement of their own in 1944 when they broke out reflective blue satin uniforms to enhance visibility during night games. The St. Louis Cardinals, Boston Braves, Cincinnati Reds and several Minor League clubs also wore the satins for a stretch.

BASEBALL PARADISE

THE CARIBBEAN WORLD Series, an annual platform for bragging rights among Latin-American baseball hotbeds, got its start in the late 1940s. It was the brainchild of Venezuelans Oscar Prieto and Pablo Morales, who conceived the concept as a follow-up to the Serie Interamericana — an annual competition featuring teams from Mexico, Cuba, Venezuela and the United States.

Cuba hosted the first Caribbean Series in 1949, and defeated entrants from Panama, Puerto Rico and Venezuela in a six-game round-robin competition. The Cubans proceeded to win seven more series crowns through 1960, when the Serie del Caribe was canceled in conjunction with Fidel Castro's decision to ban professional baseball in Cuba. But the tradition resumed in 1970, and winter league champions from the Dominican Republic, Puerto Rico, Mexico and Venezuela now engage in a spirited competition each February. Series MVP Award winners through the years include such Major League luminaries as Manny Mota, Rico Carty, Roberto Alomar and David Ortiz.

THE SHIFT

AFTER TED WILLIAMS hit three home runs and drove in eight runs in the opener of a doubleheader against Cleveland on July 14, 1946, Indians player-manager Lou Boudreau was desperate for a way to neutralize the Boston slugger. Boudreau later said that he would have stationed an outfielder in the right-field stands, "but the rules wouldn't allow that." So he decided to make up some new rules as he went along.

After Williams doubled in his first at-bat in the second game, Boudreau treated the Fenway Park crowd to some good old-fashioned innovation. As Williams stepped to the plate in his next at-bat, the Indians shifted their defense so that three players were set up to the right side of second base. Williams was so stunned, he stepped out of the batter's box and busted out laughing. He proceeded to ground out to Boudreau, Cleveland's shortstop, who had shifted to the right side of second base.

"I noticed that 95 percent of his hits or outs were to right field," Boudreau said. "He was having a carnival and that was one of the reasons we went to the extreme, hoping he

The muscular Kluszewski wore a sleeveless jersey sans undershirt to better fit his frame.

> "I NOTICED THAT 95 PERCENT OF HIS HITS OR OUTS WERE TO RIGHT FIELD." LOU BOUDREAU

THE CHANGING GAME

Boudreau's Indians were the first to use the "Williams Shift" when the skipper noticed that the Boston slugger (batting) pulled the ball 95 percent of the time he made contact.

would bunt or go the opposite way. I knew he had a great ego. If he attempted to bunt he would be conceding he couldn't go over or through the shift."

Williams, true to character, stubbornly resisted the temptation to steer the ball to the newly vacated left side. Numerous other left-handed sluggers emulated that mindset in later years.

"I'm not going to tamper with my style just to hit a few extra singles to left," Williams said. "I've spent too many years learning to pull the ball to right to take chances. If I change my style now, I might lose my power to right. I'll keep swinging away even if they put the catcher in right field."

THE OL' COLLEGE TRY

The first College World Series in 1947 featured a finals matchup between the California Golden Bears and the Yale Bulldogs. The Cal roster included pitcher-outfielder Jackie Jensen, a multi-sport athlete who played halfback on the Bears' 1949 Rose Bowl football team. He went on to enjoy a successful professional career with the Boston Red Sox and won the 1958 American League MVP Award. The Yale roster also featured some star power, but a first baseman named George Herbert Walker Bush would go on to make his name in a world beyond baseball.

Long before Bush earned acclaim as the 41st president of the United States, he was a defensively oriented first baseman at Yale. His teammates referred to him as "Poppy" and elected him captain his senior year, but he hit just .215 in three seasons with the Bulldogs.

"He was a line-drive hitter, with not too many line drives," said Ethan Allen, the former Yale coach.

Cal beat Yale, 17-4 and 8-7, at Hyames Field on the Western Michigan University campus in Kalamazoo, Mich., for the title. Bush went hitless in seven at-bats in the two games.

Yale returned to Kalamazoo the following year, but the results were equally disappointing. The Bulldogs lost two straight in a best-of-three series against Southern California and again came home empty. In the first game, Yale's Gerard Breen hit into a bases-loaded triple play in the bottom of the ninth inning — with none other than Bush standing on deck.

> BUSH WAS A DEFENSIVELY ORIENTED FIRST BASEMAN AT YALE. HIS TEAMMATES REFERRED TO HIM AS "POPPY" AND ELECTED HIM CAPTAIN HIS SENIOR YEAR.

A KID'S GAME

Carl Stotz, a young Williamsport, Pa., lumberyard clerk, was playing catch with his two nephews in the backyard in the summer of 1939 when he tripped and fell over a lilac bush. That minor stumble led to a brainstorm, and Stotz asked the boys what they would say to playing in a real league with uniforms, caps and a new ball for every game.

From those humble beginnings, an American tradition was born.

Stotz found local sponsors for teams, and Little League Baseball began play that summer with a game between Lundy Lumber and Lycoming Dairy. Eight years later, the league's board of directors gave the go-ahead for a national tournament, and the Maynard Midgets of Williamsport beat the Lock Haven All-Stars, 16-7, to capture the first-ever Little League World Series title.

Over the ensuing decades, Tom Seaver, Jim Palmer, Nolan Ryan, Mike Schmidt and dozens of other eventual Major League stars would get their start in Little League. By 2010, an estimated 2.5 million boys and girls in more than 80 countries were playing Little League baseball and softball, and the annual Little League World Series in Williamsport attracted a world-wide audience on ESPN.

Decades before he was president of the United States, Bush played first base for Yale in the College World Series.

Stotz, who died in 1992 at the age of 82, expressed amazement at how much the annual tournament in Williamsport had grown from the simple beginnings from which it originally sprang.

"Of course, I had no idea what Little League would become," Stotz said in a 1989 interview. "All I envisioned at the time was a neighborhood program."

> ### TODAY'S LITTLE LEAGUE WORLD SERIES
>
> **World Participants:** Asia-Pacific, Europe, Canada, Caribbean, Japan, Latin America, Middle-East, Africa
>
> **Format:** Two brackets — one comprised of the eight U.S. teams (Great Lakes, Midwest, Mid-Atlantic, New England, Southeast, Southwest, Northwest, West) and one comprised of the eight international teams. The tournament is double-elimination until the U.S. and International championship games, where it becomes single-elimination.
>
> **The Action:** 30 total games are played, with each team playing at least three.
>
> **Most Titles:** Chinese Taipei (17)
>
> **Ages:** 9–12, plus a Junior (13–14), Senior (14–16) and Big League (16–18) division
>
> **Primetime:** The Little League World Series airs on the ESPN family of networks (ABC, ESPN, ESPN2)

SPRING FEVER

For the better part of five decades, the Brooklyn Dodgers were well-traveled men during Spring Training. Their roster of spring homes ranged from Jacksonville, Fla., to Hot Springs, Ark., to New Orleans to Havana, Cuba. Stability finally arrived following the conclusion of World War II, when the Dodgers set up a baseball heaven in a patch of land on Florida's east coast.

In 1948, a Vero Beach businessman named Bud Holman invited the Dodgers to train in the town, and the local government did its part by turning over a vacated Naval base and accompanying barracks for the team to use. In 1952, the Dodgers invested $100,000 in the construction of Holman Stadium, complete with 1,500 chairs from Brooklyn's Ebbets Field, roofless dugouts and restrooms with "Bat Boys" and "Bat Girls" on the doors.

For the next 56 years, until the team moved to a new complex in Glendale, Ariz., in 2009, "Dodgertown" was a place for the organization's players to bond with fans and prepare for Opening Day in a quaint, self-contained environment. It had become the Fenway Park or Wrigley Field of Spring Training, a cherished ballpark that many fans were sad to see go, even if it did make more sense for a team from Los Angeles to train in the western United States. Pedestrian cross-sections bore the names of franchise greats, from Don Drysdale Drive to Sandy Koufax Lane to Roy Campanella Boulevard, and players routinely stopped to chat and sign autographs for fans while on their way to and from drills on the back fields.

For several decades, Dodgertown survived the move from Brooklyn to the West Coast, welcomed night baseball in 1968 and maintained its charm through numerous upgrades across the years.

"This is a place of greatness," Dodgers coach Manny Mota said in the spring of 2008, shortly before the team left Florida to train in Arizona. "Great history, great memories, great players, great managers and great owners."

Dodgertown quickly became a popular destination for players and fans alike.

THE WHITE HOUSE
WASHINGTON

January 15, 1942.

My dear Judge:-

Thank you for yours of January fourteenth. As you will, of course, realize the final decision about the baseball season must rest with you and the Baseball Club owners -- so what I am going to say is solely a personal and not an official point of view.

I honestly feel that it would be best for the country to keep baseball going. There will be fewer people unemployed and everybody will work longer hours and harder than ever before.

And that means that they ought to have a chance for recreation and for taking their minds off their work even more than before.

Baseball provides a recreation which does not last over two hours or two hours and a half, and which can be got for very little cost. And, incidentally, I hope that night games can be extended because it gives an opportunity to the day shift to see a game occasionally.

As to the players themselves, I know you agree with me that individual players who are of active military or naval age should go, without question, into the services. Even if the actual quality of the teams is lowered by the greater use of older players, this will not dampen the popularity of the sport. Of course, if any individual has some particular aptitude in a trade or profession, he ought to serve the Government. That, however, is a matter which I know you can handle with complete justice.

Here is another way of looking at it -- if 300 teams use 5,000 or 6,000 players, these players are a definite recreational asset to at least 20,000,000 of their fellow citizens -- and that in my judgment is thoroughly worthwhile.

With every best wish,

Very sincerely yours,

Franklin D Roosevelt

Hon. Kenesaw M. Landis,
333 North Michigan Avenue,
Chicago,
Illinois.

CHAPTER 4
BASEBALL DURING WARTIME

The onset of world-wide hostilities made for difficult choices amid baseball's fun and games. But none other than President Franklin D. Roosevelt himself decided that the game could be a source of comfort and pride in difficult times, so he gave the go-ahead for play to continue during World War II. Many Big Leaguers put personal goals aside and left their families behind to enlist in the war effort, and a young Army lieutenant named Jackie Robinson risked a court martial for refusing to go to the back of a military bus in Texas. With resources strained to the max, teams and fans alike did their part to contribute to the cause.

PRESIDENTIAL SEAL OF APPROVAL

HISTORY SHOWS THAT baseball can help people cope during times of national stress. Nearly 70 years before Mike Piazza would raise spirits at Shea Stadium with a home run in the first game in New York after the September 11 tragedy, President Franklin Roosevelt delivered a message on the power of baseball as a bonding mechanism.

A month after Japan's attack on Pearl Harbor prompted America to join its European allies in World War II, Commissioner Kenesaw Mountain Landis sent a letter to President Roosevelt asking if the 1942 Major League season would be canceled. A day later, Landis received his response. Roosevelt, at the urging of Washington Senators Owner Clark Griffith and others, endorsed the idea of going forward with the season in what came to be known as his "Green Light Letter."

"I honestly feel that it would be best for the country to keep baseball going," Roosevelt wrote. "There will be fewer people unemployed and everybody will work longer hours and harder than ever before. And that means that they ought to have a chance for recreation and for taking their minds off their work even more than before.

"Here is another way of looking at it — if 300 teams use 5,000 or 6,000 players, these players are a definite recreational asset to at least 20 million of their fellow citizens — and that in my judgment is thoroughly worthwhile."

Baseball would, indeed, proceed with play, but it was hardly business as usual. Cleveland ace Bob Feller and Detroit slugger Hank Greenberg were among the star players who quickly departed for military service, and by the time the war ended in 1945, about 500 Big Leaguers and 5,000 Minor Leaguers had joined them. Two Major Leaguers and more than 100 Minor Leaguers were killed in action, but baseball continued to provide welcome comfort to the American public for the duration of the war.

President Roosevelt's letter to Commissioner Landis demonstrated how important baseball had become to the nation's well-being.

BOY WONDER

The exodus of players to World War II battlefields in the early- to mid-1940s created roster openings that some teams went to great lengths to fill. In the summer of 1944, the Cincinnati Reds took a major leap of faith with a pitching prospect in their own backyard. Joe Nuxhall, a star athlete at Wilson Junior High in the Cincinnati suburb of Hamilton, Ohio, attracted the attention of the Reds during a late-spring tryout. The Reds actually wanted to sign his father, Orville, but the elder Nuxhall had a wife and five children to support and could ill afford to give up his job at a local auto body shop. So the Reds signed the 15-year-old Joe for a $500 bonus and $175 per month, under the provision that he stay in school and show up only for home games.

Nuxhall, to his surprise, made his debut on June 10, 1944, four days after allied troops stormed the beaches at Normandy on D-Day. With the Reds down, 13-0, against St. Louis, Cincinnati Manager Bill McKechnie called upon his young left-hander, who was so unnerved that he tripped and fell over the dugout steps on his way to the mound.

Nuxhall recorded two outs, but allowed five runs on five walks and two hits — one of them a single by Stan Musial. "I was scared to death," Nuxhall later recalled.

Nuxhall went on to spend six years in the Minors before rejoining the Reds in 1952. He posted a career 135-117 record in the Big Leagues and spent 37 years as a beloved broadcaster with the Reds before his death in 2007.

FIGHTER

Sportswriters have a soft spot for tales of ballplayers who overcome adversity during their careers. That tried-and-true storyline failed to do justice to Pete Gray, whose influence endured in a way that numbers could never convey.

Gray lost his right arm at age 6 when he fell off a farmer's delivery wagon and got pinned between the wheels. He pursued a baseball career despite his disability, and spent several productive seasons as a Minor League outfielder. In 1944, he hit .333 with 68 stolen bases for the Memphis Chicks to win the Southern League MVP Award.

Gray got his breakthrough with the St. Louis Browns in 1945 when rosters were depleted because of World War II, and went 1 for 4 against the Detroit Tigers in his Major League debut. Although Gray had difficulty hitting breaking pitches, he was fast in the field and proficient at chasing down fly balls.

Previous page: Gray proved to be more than just a novelty in his brief tenure in the Majors. This page: Nuxhall was just 15 when he made his Big League debut.

"He could outrun a scalded dog," teammate Ellis Clary said.

Some Browns players reportedly resented Gray and suspected he was called up to St. Louis as a gimmick to boost ticket sales, but Gray became a role model for disabled kids and veterans who had been injured or lost limbs in the war. After hitting .218 in 77 games in 1945, he returned to the Minors and retired four years later.

In 1986, Gray's life was chronicled in the movie, *A Winner Never Quits*. He died in his native Nanticoke, Pa., in 2002 at age 87.

OVERCOMING THE ODDS

On April 8, 1989, Yankees hurler Jim Abbott joined Pete Gray in the pantheon of one-handed Big Leaguers. And he made more history on Sept. 4, 1993, by throwing 119 pitches to record the 234th Major League no-hitter. Abbott, born without a right hand, would keep a right-handed thrower's glove on the end of his right forearm and slip it onto his left hand after releasing a pitch in order to field batted balls. The southpaw pitched 10 seasons in the Bigs for the Angels, Yankees, White Sox and Brewers, compiling an 89-108 record and a 4.25 ERA. Abbott also had a spectacular career at the University of Michigan, leading the Wolverines to two Big Ten Championships and winning the 1987 Golden Spikes Award — an honor given to the best amateur baseball player in the country. This helped propel him to a spot on the 1988 U.S. Olympic team, a squad that took home the gold medal in Seoul, South Korea.

COURAGEOUS COMEBACK

Many Major and Minor Leaguers served their country with distinction during World War II. Few of them returned from the battlefield with more compelling stories of courage than Lou Brissie.

As a youth in South Carolina, Brissie showed great promise pitching in the local textile league. He signed with the Philadelphia A's and prepared to chase his dream of pitching in the Big Leagues, but the onset of war interrupted that pursuit.

Brissie enlisted in the 88th Infantry Division of the United States Army in 1942. Two years later, he was deployed to Italy. On Dec. 7, 1944 — the third anniversary of Japan's attacks on Pearl Harbor — Brissie was in the mountains near Florence when his unit was hit by heavy fire. An artillery shell exploded and broke Brissie's left ankle and right foot and shattered his left shin bone into 30 pieces. Brissie lay in the cold for eight hours before he was finally rescued.

Doctors, fearing that gangrene would set in, considered amputating the leg, but Brissie strenuously objected.

"You can't take my leg off," Brissie told them. "I'm a ballplayer. I can't play on one leg." The doctors relented, and with diligence and penicillin, they saved Brissie's leg. He resumed his baseball career after the war and, in 1949, went 16-11 for the A's and pitched in the All-Star Game at Ebbets Field.

"There have been many stories of servicemen who barely escaped death and returned to play ball again," Grantland Rice wrote in 1948. "Lou Brissie's case puts him on top."

LIGHTS OUT

Cubs owner Philip K. Wrigley, ever the contrarian, was ready to give in to changing times in the early 1940s and install lights to bring night baseball to Wrigley Field. But those plans changed with the advent of World War II. After the Japanese attacked Pearl Harbor, Wrigley told his general manager, Jim Gallagher, to call the War Department and donate the steel meant for the light towers to the war effort.

Brissie nearly lost his leg fighting in WWII but nevertheless resumed a baseball career afterward, even making an All-Star team.

Was Wrigley's gesture a selfless act of patriotism? Perhaps, but some accounts suggested he was perfectly content to maintain the tradition of day baseball at the corner of Clark and Addison and use the donation story as a smokescreen.

"Mr. Wrigley was delighted to have an excuse to call the whole thing off," Gallagher later said. "We put a little story in the papers that the Cubs had given the steel, all the material, to a defense plant. Later, I remember asking where the steel went. I never did find out."

LET THERE BE LIGHT

Cubs Owner Philip Wrigley managed to avoid installing lights at his park in the 1940s, but the inevitable came to a reality 48 years later. The first official night game at Wrigley Field came on Aug. 9, 1988, between the Cubs and Mets, with Chicago winning, 6-4. But the hoopla over night games at Wrigley had occurred the previous evening — when rain forced the game to be called in the fourth — as the Cubs pulled out all the stops for night baseball's debut. Club icons Billy Williams and Ernie Banks threw out ceremonial first pitches. Commissioner Peter Ueberroth watched from a box seat. And 91-year-old Cubs fan Harry Grossman pulled the switch after urging the crowd to shout, "Let there be lights!"

FIRST-ROUND DRAFTEES

BASEBALL'S ELITE STARTERS frequently come with nicknames, like "Old Hoss" or "Big Train," that are testaments to their brilliance. Hugh Mulcahy, who spent most of his eight-year career with the Phillies in the 1930s and '40s, wasn't so fortunate. He posted a 42-82 record through 1940 to earn the depressing moniker of "Losing Pitcher."

But Mulcahy earned a more inspiring designation on March 8, 1941, when he became the first Big Leaguer drafted into the United States Armed Forces under the new Selective Service Act. He was assigned to the 101st Artillery Corps at Camp Edwards in Cape Cod, Mass.

This page: Wrigley remained a daytime-only ballpark when the Cubs donated steel to the war effort. Next page: Mulcahy underwhelmed on the mound, but served his country well in wartime.

BASEBALL DURING WARTIME

"I'm ready to serve," Mulcahy told a reporter. "A year away from the Big Leagues shouldn't seriously hamper my baseball career. I won't be 28 until September, and they say a pitcher's prime is between 28 and 31. So by the time I come out, I should be just reaching my peak."

Mulcahy was honorably discharged in early December after nine months of service, but his plans took an unexpected turn when the Japanese bombed Pearl Harbor. Mulcahy went back into the Army and served several more years, earning a Bronze Star before resuming his pitching career with the Phillies in 1945. He retired in 1951 with a career Big League record of 45-89.

While Mulcahy was the first pitcher drafted, Hank Greenberg held that distinction for position players. Greenberg was cleared for military service despite having flat feet, and reported for duty at Camp Custer in Michigan in May 1941. He went from a Major League–high $55,000 salary to $21 a month as an Army private. "I expect no favors," Greenberg said. "It's my duty. I'm going to be a good soldier."

THREE'S COMPANY

MAJOR LEAGUE BASEBALL teams went to great lengths to contribute to the war effort in the early 1940s. The Cincinnati Reds held a "Smokes for Servicemen" campaign in which fans brought cigarettes for the troops. And during "Waste Fat Night," the government collected grease to make soap.

Arguably the most innovative promotion took place in 1944 at the Polo Grounds, where the Brooklyn Dodgers, New York Yankees and New York Giants took part in a three-way exhibition game to help sell war bonds. The final score: Brooklyn 5, the Yankees 1 and the Giants 0.

Comedian Milton Berle and pitcher Al Schacht, the "Clown Prince of Baseball," provided the entertainment at the game, which featured numerous between-innings contests and raised more than $50 million in war bonds. Despite the positive result, the *New York Times* concluded that the event "won the lunacy championship hands down."

CALL OF DUTY

BOB FELLER NEVER lacked for assertiveness as a star pitcher with the Cleveland Indians. He reacted even more decisively when the fun and games ended and his patriotism was put to the test.

By December 1941 Feller was just 23 years old, but already had 107 victories to his credit. He was driving from his home in Iowa to Chicago for contract negotiations when news broke that the Japanese had attacked the United States naval base in Pearl Harbor, Hawaii.

Feller's father was dying of cancer and, as his family's sole wage earner, he could have qualified for a draft deferment. But he immediately volunteered for duty, and was sworn in by former boxing champion Gene Tunney, the Navy's advisor on physical fitness.

Feller went on to amass a distinguished record as a chief petty officer aboard USS Alabama. He earned eight battle stars while overseeing an 18-man gunnery crew.

Feller missed three seasons from 1942–44 and all but nine starts in 1945. The extended absence left him 34 wins short of 300, but he never lamented his time away from the ball field. Until his death at age 92, Feller chose to refer to himself as a "survivor" rather than a "hero."

"I can look anybody in the eye who was in the war, whether they're wearing a Congressional Medal of Honor or a Purple Heart," Feller said in a 1990 interview. "I was there, but I was no hero. I just did the job every good American should have done."

THE DIVIDING LINE

SPRING TRAINING IS traditionally a time for baseball teams to head for warm-weather climates. But with railroad lines strained to the max carrying troops and supplies, the landscape changed significantly during World War II. A *Sporting News* editorial called for a Spring Training and regular season "devoid of frills," which led to teams limiting their travel and preparing much closer to home.

Not legally bound to serve, Feller willingly gave up some prime years to join the Navy.

An agreement between Commissioner Kenesaw Mountain Landis and Joseph Eastman, head of the Federal Office of Defense Transportation, established the parameters: Except for the two Chicago and two St. Louis teams, who were allowed to train in Missouri, Indiana or Illinois, all other clubs were confined to an area north of the Potomac and Ohio rivers and east of the Mississippi.

The Landis-Eastman Line, or Potomac Line, as it was also called, remained in effect for three more years, after which the commissioner lifted the restrictions and teams returned to training in warm-weather locales.

DOUBLE DUTY

Bob Feller, Ted Williams and other future Hall of Famers were widely hailed for their contributions to the Allied forces during World War II. Morris "Moe" Berg, a career .243-hitting catcher with the Red Sox, White Sox and three other clubs, made his mark with a more secretive legacy.

Berg, a product of Princeton University and Columbia Law School, was an acclaimed renaissance man with a knowledge of advanced physics and Egyptian hieroglyphics and had the ability to speak 12 languages. He made a name for himself in 1939 while answering obscure trivia questions on the popular radio show *Information Please!*

"He was as smart a player that ever came along," Casey Stengel said. "It was amazing how he got all that knowledge and used them penetrating words, but he never put on too strong. They thought he was like me — a bit eccentric."

As the son of Ukrainian Jews who emigrated to New York, Berg also had a personal stake in helping to stop the rise of Adolf Hitler. As told in the 1995 book, *The Catcher Was a Spy: The Mysterious Life of Moe Berg*, he put his skills to use as a U.S. spy during World War II.

Berg joined the Office of Strategic Services, the predecessor to the CIA, in 1943, and went on spying missions throughout Europe. In 1944 he traveled undercover to Switzerland for a lecture by scientist Werner Heisenberg, and had instructions to shoot Heisenberg if he determined the Germans were close to developing an atomic bomb. But Berg found that wasn't the case, and never followed through with the assassination plot.

THE ARMY LEAGUE

While much of the premier Major League talent was overseas, a drop in quality of play was inevitable. But the top players kept their skills sharp by participating in the Army League, which was highlighted by such Big League stars as Ted Williams, Joe DiMaggio, Stan Musial and Joe Gordon, each of whom would later be inducted into the Hall of Fame.

This talent boon in the Army League did not go unnoticed, either. The Service World Series, a series between the Army and Navy, garnered significant interest as fans flocked to see the competition. Crowds of 40,000 came to each game to watch their favorite players, even if they weren't playing for their favorite teams.

TRAGIC LOSSES

Eiji Sawamura made a lasting impression as a 17-year-old high school pitcher, striking out Charlie Gehringer, Babe Ruth, Lou Gehrig and Jimmie Foxx in succession during an exhibition game against a Major League All-Star squad in Japan. But Sawamura's promising baseball career ended much too soon.

After pitching three no-hitters and posting a 63-22 record for the Yomiuri Giants, Sawamura enlisted in the Japanese Imperial Navy in 1943. He died the following year, at just 27 years of age, when his transport ship was struck by a torpedo near the Ryukyu Islands off the coast of Taiwan. Sawamura was inducted into the Japanese Baseball Hall of Fame in 1959, and the award given annually to the best pitcher in Japan's Nippon Professional Baseball League bears his name.

Masaru Kageura, an accomplished hitter for the Osaka Tigers and one of Sawamura's most respected rivals, also met his fate in action during World War II in the Battle of the Philippines. He was honored with his own Hall of Fame plaque in 1965.

One of the smartest Major Leaguers to ever grace a diamond, Berg put his intelligence to good use as a spy during WWII.

CIVIL RIGHTS

JACKIE ROBINSON'S INFLUENCE as a racial trailblazer preceded his exploits on the baseball diamond. Three years before breaking Major League Baseball's color barrier by signing with the Brooklyn Dodgers — and 11 years before Rosa Parks refused to give up her seat on a city bus in Montgomery, Ala. — Robinson made an eloquent statement to advance the cause of integration.

In 1944, while serving as a lieutenant in the 761st Tank Battalion at Fort Hood, Texas, Robinson refused to move to the back of an Army bus. He was on solid ground, given the Army's new prohibition against racial segregation. But he was nevertheless arrested, charged with insubordination and court-martialed.

The Army was understandably anxious about a backlash in support of Robinson, who was well-known from his days as a star multisport athlete at UCLA. In a three-page letter to Truman Gibson, a civilian aide to the Secretary of War, Robinson wondered if he might not be best-served telling newspapers about the trumped-up charges against him in order to help advance his cause. "I don't mind trouble, but I do believe in fair play and justice," Robinson wrote.

In the end, it took a panel of nine officers four days to acquit Robinson of the charges. Robinson received a transfer to Camp Breckenridge in Kentucky, where he coached athletics teams before receiving an honorable discharge from the Army. He joined the Kansas City Monarchs in the Negro Leagues in 1945, and debuted in the Major Leagues two years later.

A LEAGUE OF THEIR OWN

WHILE DEPLETED ROSTERS forced clubs to consider teenagers and other marginally talented fill-ins during World War II, an even more surprising contingent stepped to the forefront: Women became a baseball staple in the mid-1940s.

The All-American Girls Professional Baseball League, the brainchild of Chicago Cubs Owner Philip Wrigley, was born in 1943 as a means of selling tickets at the ballpark in the event that interest in the Major Leagues waned with the exodus of star players to the battlefield. It began as a softball league, with shortened bases and pitchers throwing underhand, before overhand pitching and smaller ball sizes were adopted.

Hall of Famers Jimmie Foxx and Max Carey signed on as managers in the AAGPBL — memorably, a movie was made about it in 1992 called *A League of Their Own* — which was made up of clubs in cities throughout the Midwest. The Kenosha Comets, Racine Belles, Rockford Peaches and South Bend Blue Sox began play in 1943, and were soon joined by the Milwaukee Chicks, Minneapolis Millerettes, Fort Wayne Daisies and Grand Rapids Chicks.

Between practices and games, the ballplayers received tips on etiquette and proper hygiene. They each received a beauty kit and attended charm school classes overseen by Helena Rubenstein's beauty salon.

"Especially after the game, the All-American girl should take time to observe the necessary beauty ritual, to protect both her health and appearance," they were told in their introductory primer.

But the women played with a skill and fervor that resonated with fans. Art Meyerhoff, Wrigley's Chicago advertising director, worked to maintain a high standard of play after taking over the league's operations in 1944.

"Maybe at first the men came out to see the legs," said Pepper Paire Davis, a star shortstop and catcher in the AAGPBL for 10 seasons. "But they stuck around when they realized they were seeing a darn good brand of baseball."

Robinson's courage against racial discrimination during the war portended things to come, as he would later break the Major League color barrier.

BASEBALL DURING WARTIME

The Rockford Peaches, part of the All-American Girls Professional Baseball League, pose in 1943.

CHAPTER 5
IN THE FRONT OFFICE

While Judge Kenesaw Mountain Landis's death paved the way for a new commissioner, innovation was the order of the day in front offices throughout the game. Bill Veeck conceived a variety of novel promotions in Cleveland, and Branch Rickey's influence went well beyond his role as a racial trailblazer in Brooklyn. Downstairs in the dugout, Casey Stengel proved that first impressions aren't always as they seem. Derided by many as overmatched, Stengel quickly found his stride as manager of baseball's most hallowed franchise. The "Old Perfessor" joined the Yankees in 1949 and helped perpetuate a dynasty in the Bronx.

RICKEY'S BLUNDER

JOHNNY MIZE'S MOST astonishing achievement on a baseball field came during the 1947 season with the New York Giants, when he led the National League with 51 home runs while striking out just 42 times. Mize possessed a rare combination of power and plate discipline that prompted teammates and opponents to view him with a sense of reverence.

Skipper Casey Stengel — who was helming the Brooklyn Dodgers in 1936 when Mize broke into the Majors with the Cards — called Mize a slugger who hit like a leadoff man, and Stan Musial considered him "one of the best hitters ever."

"Sure, we know how to pitch to him. But when you're squatting back of Mr. Mize, his bat swells up," observed Dodgers catching great Roy Campanella.

Having steadily built a reputation as one of baseball's top power hitters during the late 1930s, Mize eventually found himself at loggerheads with the notoriously thrifty Branch Rickey, then St. Louis's general manager. According to several accounts, Mize was displeased when Rickey wanted to cut his salary despite Mize's home run total increasing from 28 in 1939 to 43 in 1940, but Rickey pointed out that his batting average had dipped from .349 to .314.

Rickey finally resolved the dispute by sending Mize to the Giants for $50,000 and three nondescript players. In the annals of Cardinals history, the Mize trade will be remembered as one of Rickey's greatest blunders. Mize went on to hit 359 career home runs and make the Hall of Fame, and Musial later described the trade as a "terrible mistake."

Despite establishing himself as one of the best hitters in the Majors, Mize (left) was sold by Cardinals GM Rickey to the Giants in the prime of his career after a salary dispute.

IN THE FRONT OFFICE

LADIES FIRST

As the driving force behind the Newark Eagles of the Negro Leagues in the 1930s and '40s, Effa Manley handled player transactions, conducted contract negotiations, cut the checks and was responsible for every significant baseball and business decision the organization made.

A confident, assertive woman who held her own in an overwhelmingly masculine industry, she also struck a blow for equality of race and gender that would eventually land her a place in Cooperstown.

Born to white parents, Manley grew up in a bi-racial environment in Philadelphia. She married African-American businessman Abe Manley in 1935, and they formed the Brooklyn Eagles of the Negro National League, soon merging the club with the Newark Dodgers and shifting the team's operations to New Jersey.

Effa quickly developed a reputation as a shrewd, strong-willed businesswoman and an advocate for player and civil rights. She held a firm line in contract talks, but also required her ballplayers to dress well and act like professionals in the event the Major Leagues came calling. She replaced the Newark team's rickety bus with an air-conditioned, $15,000 Flxible Clipper bus, and sponsored a team in the Puerto Rican winter leagues to ensure the players had work in the offseason.

Manley was also active in the Newark branch of the NAACP, holding an "anti-lynching day" at Ruppert Stadium in 1939. Former Eagles Monte Irvin, Larry Doby, Ray Dandridge, Leon Day and Willie Wells all made it to the Baseball Hall of Fame, and Manley joined them in 2006 when she became the first woman enshrined in Cooperstown. Her gravestone carries the succinct inscription, "She Loved Baseball."

SEND IN THE CLOWN

Baseball fans in the Big Apple first came to know Casey Stengel from his days as a modestly talented yet immoderately talkative outfielder with the Brooklyn Dodgers from 1912–17. What Stengel may have lacked in skill, he more than made up for in crowd-pleasing ability. While visiting Ebbets Field with the Pittsburgh Pirates in 1919 — and with Brooklyn fans taunting him — Stengel tipped his cap to the crowd and a sparrow flew out from beneath it, transforming the boos to cheers.

Not long after his playing career ended, Stengel graduated to managing the Dodgers, but his reputation as the fun-loving type never waned. In 1949, when New York Yankees General Manager George Weiss brought up Stengel's name as a managerial candidate, co-owner Del Webb made his opposition eminently clear. "He's a clown," Webb reportedly shouted. "I don't want a clown managing the New York Yankees."

Weiss patiently explained that Stengel's buffoonish persona was overblown — that he was instead a dedicated, knowledgeable baseball man who had a great mind for the game. At this point, Stengel hadn't managed since a partial-season stint with the Boston Braves in 1943. Webb finally agreed to sign off on the move if his partner, Dan Topping, also approved the hiring.

Shortly thereafter, the Yankees held a press conference at the swanky 21 Club in Manhattan to introduce their new manager. When Stengel stepped before the microphone and thanked "Mr. *Bob* Topping" for the opportunity, things appeared to be off to a shaky start.

CASEY STENGEL'S MANAGERIAL CAREER

Team	Years Managed	Record
Brooklyn Dodgers	1934–36	208-251
Boston Braves	1938–43	373-491
New York Yankees	1949–60	1,149-696
New York Mets	1962–65	175-404

The highly respected Manley helped pave the way for both racial and gender equality in baseball.

More than just a crowd-pleaser, Stengel (left) managed the Yankees to seven world titles and 10 pennants.

IN THE FRONT OFFICE

Luckily for Stengel, first impressions were meaningless in this case. After posting a nondescript record of 581-742 in his first two stops in Brooklyn and Boston, Stengel flourished in the Bronx. Over the next 12 seasons, he guided the Yankees to 10 American League pennants, seven championships and a .623 winning percentage. By the end, nobody was calling him a clown anymore.

SHOWMAN

BILL VEECK WAS 32 years old when he assembled a syndicate that bought the Cleveland Indians in 1946. He spent only three and a half years in Cleveland, but his time in the Cuyahoga Valley was notable for winning teams and mammoth crowds. What was the secret to his success?

In his autobiography, *Veeck As In Wreck*, the innovative baseball lifer explained, "We drew our crowds in the following unheroic, sweaty ways: 1) We gave them a lot of fun and a lot of entertainment; 2) I hit the Chautauqua Trail, making as many as 500 speeches a year; 3) We built a winning team."

INDIANS ATTENDANCE UNDER VEECK, 1946–49

Year	Attendance	AL Rank
1946	1,057,289	4 of 8
1947	1,521,978	2 of 8
1948	2,620,627	1 of 8
1949	2,233,771	2 of 8

In 1948, the Tribe won the American League pennant, beat the Braves in the World Series and set a single-season attendance record of 2,620,627. Fans flocked to Municipal Stadium to see Bob Feller, Joe Gordon and other stars, but Veeck took nothing for granted. He was energetic and imaginative in his promotions, and never rested in his quest to increase gate receipts.

The Indians treated crowds to fireworks displays and circus acts, and Veeck hired two in-house entertainers, Max Patkin and Jackie Price. He gave female fans orchids when they passed through the gates, and set up an on-site babysitting service at the park.

When Joe Early, a night watchman at a Chevrolet plant, wrote a letter to the editor of the *Cleveland Press* asking why baseball teams never have special nights for the average Joe, Veeck obliged. The Indians invited Early to a game and gave him a Ford convertible, a refrigerator and a washing machine, and a truck full of other gifts in conjunction with "Good Old Joe Early Night."

DESERT BASEBALL

WHILE SHIFTING HIS team's Spring Training operation from Florida to Arizona in 1947 may have given Cleveland Indians Owner Bill Veeck the opportunity to spend February and March at his Tucson ranch, Veeck was thinking about more than creature comforts and the therapeutic effects of a dry heat when he moved the Indians westward.

Veeck had plans to sign an African-American player, and he thought fans and local businesses in Arizona might be more hospitable to the idea than those in Florida. His suspicions were confirmed when standout Negro Leagues outfielder Larry Doby became the American League's first black player. Doby made his spring debut for the Indians in 1948 and was greeted with loud ovations during both trips to the plate in his first game, according to the *Arizona Republic*.

Horace Stoneham's New York Giants accompanied Veeck's Indians to Tucson in 1947. When the Chicago Cubs and Baltimore Orioles set up shop in Arizona in the early '50s, a new spring circuit, appropriately dubbed the "Cactus League," was born.

Veeck was an unconventional owner, but his methods helped make the Indians one of the biggest draws in the Major Leagues.

IN THE FRONT OFFICE

ON THE FARM

BEFORE THE 1920 season, Branch Rickey and the St. Louis Cardinals purchased the contract of a promising 24-year-old Minor League knuckleballer named Jesse Haines from the Cincinnati Reds for $10,000. The right-handed Haines had appeared in just one game for the Reds during the 1918 season and had spent all of the 1919 campaign toiling in the Minors. Cardinals Owner Sam Breadon had to borrow the money from a bank to allow the transaction to take place.

From that single, unassuming deal, a sweeping change in the way that teams developed talent was born.

"What Rickey was about to propose was revolutionary," wrote biographer Murray Polner. "He was going to build a network of affiliated Minor League teams, a development with such far-reaching implications that it ultimately and dramatically changed St. Louis and, later, all of baseball."

"Later" came during the 1940s, when the Cardinals and Brooklyn Dodgers relied on strong, homegrown talent to churn out a succession of winning ballclubs. The more promising young players Rickey signed and developed internally, the more difficult it was for opponents — who were mostly focused on acquiring established stars — to get their hands on that haul. It wasn't long before teams throughout the game began to emulate his recipe for success.

HAPPY TIMES

OWNERS THROUGHOUT MAJOR League Baseball were searching for a strong, authoritative voice when they named Kenesaw Mountain Landis as the game's first commissioner in the aftermath of the infamous 1919 Black Sox scandal. A former federal judge who was appointed by President Theodore Roosevelt, Landis vigorously and immediately exercised the powers of his new office, banning superstar "Shoeless" Joe Jackson and seven other White Sox in 1921 for conspiring with gamblers to throw the '19 World Series to the Cincinnati Reds.

Upon Landis's death in 1944, the owners replaced him with Albert Benjamin "Happy" Chandler, a former governor and United States Senator from Kentucky. Aptly named for his typically jovial nature, Chandler established himself as a friend to the players.

During his term, Chandler oversaw the development of a players' pension fund, made headlines for suspending Dodgers Manager Leo Durocher for associating with gamblers and endorsed the concept of integration in baseball. Chandler's public support of integrated baseball, despite the reluctance of several team owners and no small part of baseball's fan community, helped make Jackie Robinson's debut with the Brooklyn Dodgers in 1947 possible.

"I believe this is a free country and everybody should have a chance to play," Chandler said in May 1945, several months before the Dodgers signed Robinson to break baseball's color barrier. In the face of opposition to Robinson's participation in the Major Leagues, Chandler seemed to become a champion for underdogs of all shapes and sizes. He — along with other key figures, such as Branch Rickey — stood their ground in the face of it all, and baseball has reaped the rewards as a result.

"We Americans are a peculiar people," Chandler said. "We are for the underdog, no matter how much of a dog he is."

In the end, some baseball owners deemed Chandler too independent, and he failed to gain re-election to a second term in 1951. But his contributions were recognized in 1982 with his election to the Baseball Hall of Fame.

As commissioner, Chandler was a friend of the players, helping to establish their pension fund while also promoting integration.

CHAPTER 6
INTEGRATION

Pennant races and championship celebrations pale in comparison to the societal upheaval that took place in the 1940s. Branch Rickey made a bold move to integrate the Brooklyn Dodgers, and he picked the right player in Jackie Robinson. Bill Veeck jumped into the fray soon after, signing Larry Doby in Cleveland, and by the early 1950s more than 150 former Negro Leagues players had made the transition to Major League clubs. Through the courage they displayed in their historic "partnership," Rickey and Robinson forever changed the face of the game. Beginning in 2004, MLB celebrates Robinson's legacy every April 15 with Jackie Robinson Day, in which Big Leaguers wear the No. 42 in his honor.

TRAILBLAZER

THE GROUNDWORK FOR one of the seminal events in baseball history was laid during a secret meeting at a spartanly furnished office on Montague Street in Brooklyn. That's where Dodgers General Manager Branch Rickey summoned Jackie Robinson to gain the measure of the man who would be the focal point of his "noble experiment" to integrate Major League Baseball.

Accompanied by Dodgers scout Clyde Sukeforth, Robinson arrived in New York by train for the meeting on Aug. 28, 1945. The pair sat in Rickey's office, which had a goldfish tank in one corner and portraits of Abraham Lincoln and Dodgers Manager Leo Durocher hanging on the wall. The mood was initially tense as Rickey and Robinson stared silently and tried to get a read on one another.

Rickey, holding a cigar, "peered at Robinson as if he were looking through the young man's dark brown skin and into the depths of his soul, as if he could foretell his future," wrote author Jonathan Eig in his book, *Opening Day*.

After some small talk, Rickey plunged into the heart of the matter: He wanted to bring a black player to Brooklyn, but he knew what obstacles awaited, so he had to make sure that Robinson had the proper temperament to handle the ordeal. Rickey pulled out a copy of Giovanni Papini's *Life of Christ* and read a passage on non-resistance.

Did Robinson have the intestinal fortitude to turn the other cheek — potentially for years — amid a steady barrage of taunts and abusive treatment? When Robinson made it clear he was ready, the deal was done: He would receive a $3,500 signing bonus and a monthly salary of $600.

Ever ahead of the times, Rickey's signing of Robinson proved a boon to both the Civil Rights Movement and to the Major Leagues.

Soon afterward, Robinson filled out a questionnaire from the American Baseball Bureau, a public relations firm. When asked to describe his career ambition, he replied: "To open the door for Negroes in Organized Ball."

BREAKING THROUGH

THE APRIL AIR was crisp and the sky cloudless and clear on the day of Jackie Robinson's first Major League game in 1947. Robinson and Branch Rickey, the Brooklyn Dodgers' visionary president and general manager, both grasped the importance of the moment, but they were apparently in the minority. No camera bulbs flashed in recognition of Robinson breaking baseball's color barrier, and about 5,800 of the 32,500 available seats at Ebbets Field were left unfilled.

Outfielder Pete Reiser's two-run double to right field helped the Dodgers earn a 5-3 victory over the Boston Braves that day. Robinson played flawless defense, but went hitless in three at-bats. He grounded out in the first inning, flied to left field in the third and hit into a double play in the fifth before reaching on an error in the seventh inning after laying down a sacrifice bunt.

Although the veteran scribes in the press box were aware of the ramifications of Robinson's debut, the event was generally an afterthought in the following day's newspapers. The *New York Times* columnist Arthur Daley described Robinson's debut as "quite uneventful," waiting until the 10th paragraph of his game account to mention it. "The muscular Negro minds his own business and shrewdly makes no effort to push himself," Daley wrote. "He speaks quietly and intelligently when spoken to and already has made a strong impression."

Over the next 150 games, Robinson proved beyond a shadow of a doubt that he belonged in the Major Leagues. He hit .297 with 12 home runs and 29 stolen bases to win baseball's Rookie of the Year Award over pitcher Larry Jansen, who won 21 games for the New York Giants. In 1987, four decades after Robinson took the field in Brooklyn, the National and American Leagues renamed the top rookie honor the "Jackie Robinson Award" in his memory.

EYE FOR TALENT

CLYDE LEROY SUKEFORTH grew up in rural Maine in the early 1900s, before the days of radio and television. The newspaper was his lifeline to the baseball world, and he frequently scoured the box scores for updates on his favorite team, the Boston Red Sox, and his favorite player, Babe Ruth.

Sukeforth eventually left his hometown of Washington, Maine, for a stint at Georgetown University in Washington, D.C. He played in the Big Leagues with the Cincinnati Reds and Brooklyn Dodgers, but was never the same after suffering an eye injury in a 1931 hunting accident.

Sukeforth's friends and neighbors back home knew him as the modest, affable "Sukey." In baseball circles, he's remembered as the behind-the-scenes facilitator to one of the pivotal events in the game's history.

In 1945, Brooklyn General Manager Branch Rickey dispatched Sukeforth, by then his top talent evaluator, to Chicago to check out a young Negro Leagues infielder named Jackie Robinson. Robinson was unable to play because of an arm injury, so Sukeforth bought him a train ticket, accompanied him to Brooklyn and arranged the meeting with Rickey that was a prelude to Robinson's breaking the game's color barrier.

Robinson's debut passed without much fanfare, but he would go on to win the 1947 Rookie of the Year Award.

Unhappily, it wasn't Sukeforth's only brush with fame. In October 1951, Sukeforth was Brooklyn's bullpen coach in the finale of a three-game playoff between the Dodgers and Giants. When Brooklyn Manager Charlie Dressen called down to the 'pen to ask whether to bring in Carl Erskine or Ralph Branca, Sukeforth suggested Branca — who promptly gave up Bobby Thomson's famous "Shot Heard 'Round the World."

BEFORE THE BIG SHOW

JACKIE ROBINSON'S DEBUT with the Brooklyn Dodgers transcended baseball and changed society. But in the narrative arc of Robinson's career, it was merely the opening game in a watershed doubleheader.

Before Brooklyn there was Montreal, and Robinson's coming-out party with the Dodgers' International League farm club. On April 18, 1946, before a crowd of 25,000 at Roosevelt Stadium in Jersey City, N.J., Robinson went 4 for 5 with four runs scored, three RBI and two stolen bases.

Dodgers General Manager Branch Rickey prepared Robinson for his big day by urging the second baseman to be aggressive. "Run those bases like lightning," Rickey told Robinson. "I want you to worry the daylights out of those pitchers. Don't be afraid to steal that extra base."

Robinson tormented the Jersey City Giants with his wide-ranging skills in a 14-1 Montreal victory. He homered in his second plate appearance, bunted for a hit his next time up and wreaked havoc on the bases all day with his speed. When the game was complete, Robinson was besieged for autographs, and the newspaper accounts were filled with praise.

"The most significant sports story of the century was written into the record books," Joe Bostic wrote in the *Amsterdam News*. "Baseball took up the cudgel for democracy and an unassuming Negro boy ascended the heights of excellence to prove the righteousness of the experiment."

In 1998, a statue was dedicated in Robinson's honor in Jersey City's Journal Square. Echoing Robinson's personal mantra, the inscription reads: "A life is not important except in the impact it has on other lives."

> "AN UNASSUMING NEGRO BOY ASCENDED THE HEIGHTS OF EXCELLENCE TO PROVE THE RIGHTEOUSNESS OF THE EXPERIMENT." JOE BOSTIC

FELLER'S RECRUITS

AS IF 266 career victories, three no-hitters and a record of distinguished World War II service weren't enough to complete his resume, Cleveland pitcher Bob Feller struck a major blow for racial equality in the 1940s.

Feller organized a barnstorming tour in 1946, featuring players from the Negro Leagues and Major League Baseball. He enlisted the help of Satchel Paige, a natural showman and crowd pleaser.

"Feller and Paige were an unlikely twosome," wrote author Larry Tye. "Rapid Robert was as stiff and awkward as Ol' Satchel was playful and charming. Feller came of age in the Iowa cornfields, Satchel in an Alabama ghetto."

Feller recruited Stan Musial, Phil Rizzuto, Johnny Sain and numerous other stars for his squad, while Paige's roster included the likes of Hilton Smith, Monte Irvin and Buck O'Neil. Feller chartered two planes for the clubs, and scheduled 35 games throughout the country.

Feller's motivation was primarily financial, and he succeeded on that front. The tour drew 250,000 fans and generated a lucrative payout for the players. But the wrangling over gate receipts ultimately produced some hard feelings; Paige claimed that he didn't receive the money he was owed, and he sued Feller for $3,800. The dispute prompted Feller to replace the Paige All-Stars with a group led by Jackie Robinson. Still, Feller's brainstorm was acclaimed as a success on multiple fronts.

"Feller's '46 tour left a huge legacy — and not just the one in Bob's bank account," wrote author Timothy Gay. "Most important, Feller gave sorely needed exposure to black-ball and its artisans."

Feller's barnstorming tour in 1946 was a success thanks to the use of both Major Leaguers and Negro Leagues players.

NOT QUITE READY

THREE MONTHS AFTER Jackie Robinson made his debut with the Brooklyn Dodgers, the St. Louis Browns signed a pair of Negro Leagues hitters: outfielder Willard Brown and second baseman Hank Thompson of the Kansas City Monarchs. The signings were meant to give the woebegone Browns a boost both on the field and at the gate, but the experiment had barely begun when it was written off as a miserable failure.

St. Louis, the southernmost Major League team at the time, was by most accounts not ready for an integrated roster. Brown, one of the Negro Leagues' premier sluggers, had the talent to compete in the Major Leagues, but allegedly alienated teammates and fans with his questionable effort and indifferent demeanor.

According to some news accounts, Brown took his position with a copy of *Reader's Digest* in his pocket so he would have something to occupy his time during breaks in the game action. He also displayed less than maximum energy, routinely walking on and off the field. But Buck O'Neil, Brown's former manager in Kansas City, said his reputation for half-hearted play was unfair.

"Willard had so much ability, he made it look easy," O'Neil said. "People might think he was loafing, but he was a great natural athlete who never looked like he was in a hurry unless he had to be."

Whatever the reason, things failed to pan out for both Negro Leagues acquisitions in St. Louis. Thompson hit .256 in 27 games, Brown batted .179 in 21 games, and the Browns cut their ties with both players before the end of August.

> "WILLARD HAD SO MUCH ABILITY, HE MADE IT LOOK EASY. PEOPLE MIGHT THINK HE WAS LOAFING, BUT HE WAS A GREAT NATURAL ATHLETE WHO NEVER LOOKED LIKE HE WAS IN A HURRY UNLESS HE HAD TO BE." BUCK O'NEIL

PITCHING IN

DAN BANKHEAD, ONE of five baseball-playing brothers from Empire, Ala., crashed through a racial barrier in August 1947 when he became the first African-American pitcher to appear in a Major League game.

Historically speaking, the appearance was significant; aesthetically, it was a disaster. Just a few months after Jackie Robinson's debut with the Dodgers, Brooklyn General Manager Branch Rickey signed Bankhead, a successful hurler with the Memphis Red Sox in the Negro Leagues. Rickey compared Bankhead to former Cardinals star Dizzy Dean, and others labeled him the "next Satchel Paige."

Bankhead's first appearance failed to live up to those glowing reviews. Summoned to pitch in relief during a game against Pittsburgh, Bankhead allowed six runs on 10 hits in 3.1 innings. He cited fatigue from his busy Memphis workload as a factor in his performance, and some observers took note that he was clearly nervous on the mound.

Bankhead, also an excellent hitter, salvaged some pride with his bat, launching a home run into the center-field bleachers against the Pirates' Fritz Ostermueller in his first Big League plate appearance.

Bankhead became the Majors' first African-American pitcher just months after Robinson's debut.

Thompson (far left) and Brown (right), sitting with Browns Manager Muddy Ruel in 1947, didn't last long in the Big Leagues.

The rest of the season was a washout for Bankhead, and he returned to the Minor Leagues to regroup before getting another shot with Brooklyn in 1950. Bankhead posted a 9-4 record with a 5.50 ERA, but midseason shoulder problems brought an end to his pitching career, and he spent the next dozen years or so as a position player in the Mexican League. He died of cancer in 1976, one day before his 56th birthday.

THE JUNIOR CIRCUIT'S TURN

IN HIS AUTOBIOGRAPHY, *Veeck As In Wreck*, Bill Veeck reflected upon an audacious plan that he hatched in 1943 that would have set the baseball establishment on its ear: Several years before Jackie Robinson broke the color barrier with the Brooklyn Dodgers, Veeck wanted to buy the Philadelphia Phillies and stock the roster with African-American players.

Decades later, baseball historians disputed Veeck's claims and called the veracity of the plan into question. But there was no denying that Veeck, in his position as Cleveland Indians owner, played a significant role in the move toward integration in baseball.

In early July 1947, with Robinson's Brooklyn debut in full swing, Veeck contacted Newark Eagles Owner Effa Manley with a proposition: He offered her $10,000 for the rights to outfielder Larry Doby and promised to sweeten the deal by $5,000, "if we keep him." The two clubs agreed on terms, and within days Doby was on a train to Chicago for a series between the Indians and the White Sox.

Doby made his Big League debut on July 5 — 81 days after Robinson broke the color barrier — and went on to a successful career with the Indians, White Sox and Tigers. He hit .283 with 253 home runs and made it into the Baseball Hall of Fame through the Veterans Committee in 1998.

Doby endured many of the same taunts and personal slights that Robinson lived through, and was forced to stay in separate hotels from his teammates on the road. But if he felt slighted over receiving less recognition than Robinson, he never showed it.

"Why should I get more publicity than Mr. Robinson?" Doby said in a 1997 interview. "Mr. Robinson was first, so why should I get more? I've never known of the second person to get more than the first person."

HOLDING HIS OWN

Bill Veeck may be remembered for some bizarre antics — like sending 3-foot-7 Eddie Gaedel to the plate in a 1951 game — but the one that made the most sense might have been his decision to sign Larry Doby.

In addition to breaking the color barrier in the American League, Doby was one heck of a player for Cleveland. He went on to have a 13-season career in which he collected 1,515 hits and 253 home runs. In his first full season in 1948, Doby recorded an OPS of .873. The next year, he made the All-Star team, the first of seven straight selections. And in 1949, he led the league in OBP (.442) and OPS (.986) while finishing eighth in MVP voting.

The Indians, in turn, excelled. In 1954, Doby led his club to an AL-best 111 wins and finished second in the MVP voting after slamming an American League–best 32 home runs and leading the league with 126 RBI. The future Hall of Famer also won a World Series championship with Cleveland in 1948, batting .318 with a .375 OBP in six games against the Braves.

SOUTH OF THE BORDER

THE MAJORS SHUT their doors to black players until Jackie Robinson broke the color barrier in 1947. Before and after that groundbreaking event, many Negro Leaguers found a more welcoming environment south of the U.S.

Satchel Paige, Cool Papa Bell and Josh Gibson were among the prominent black players who left the United States for the Mexican League before World War II. In 1940, Bell won the league's triple crown with a .437 batting average, 12 home runs and 79 RBI. The following year, Gibson went deep 33 times to easily break the Mexican League home run record.

Doby didn't get the same attention as Robinson, but he played a crucial role in integrating the Majors while producing Hall-of-Fame numbers.

INTEGRATION

Many African-American ballplayers found equality playing in the Mexican League.

Baseball's black players also reveled in their newfound sense of equality in Mexico. "I was branded a Negro in the States and had to act accordingly. Everything I did, including playing ball, was regulated by my color," said shortstop Willie Wells. "Here, in Mexico, I am a man."

DEATH OF THE NEGRO LEAGUES

With the arrival of Jackie Robinson, Larry Doby, Satchel Paige and other prominent black ballplayers, Major League Baseball celebrated a renaissance at the ticket window. African-American fans began following the Brooklyn Dodgers in droves, and National League attendance passed the 10 million–fan barrier in 1947. The following season, with Doby and the Cleveland Indians leading the way, the American League topped 11 million at the gates.

But integration also changed the dynamic in a way that spelled death for one longtime baseball tradition: With the elimination of the color barrier, the Negro Leagues were living on borrowed time.

By 1952, more than 150 former Negro Leaguers were playing for Major League clubs, and both the Negro American and National Leagues were forced to disband. Although the Kansas City Monarchs and other teams played to large, raucous and devoted crowds during the war years of the 1940s, a watershed event in Brooklyn led to a baseball revolution, and just like that, the Negro Leagues were only a memory.

Previous page: Gibson made his living in both the Negro Leagues and Mexican League.
This page: Doby's Big League debut was pioneering, but also signaled the demise of the Negro Leagues.

CHAPTER 7

AMAZING ROOKIE SEASONS

Jackie Robinson made such a profound impact on the game in his debut season with the Brooklyn Dodgers in 1947 that Major League Baseball eventually renamed its Rookie of the Year Award in his honor. But Robinson wasn't the only phenom to capture the imagination of the baseball writers who handed out the award in the decade. Some rookies, like Stan "The Man" Musial and Richie Ashburn, showed exceptional staying power on their way to the Hall of Fame in Cooperstown. Others, such as Dick Wakefield, Johnny Beazley and Gene Bearden, defined the term "flash in the pan"; their moment in the sun was all too fleeting.

FROM BOY TO 'THE MAN'

IN THE SUMMER of 1942, the St. Louis Cardinals won a franchise-record 106 games to outlast the Brooklyn Dodgers for the National League pennant. Then they beat the New York Yankees in five games to celebrate their third championship in 12 seasons. It was also the year that St. Louis welcomed a sweet-swinging, harmonica-playing phenom who would soon become known as "The Man."

Stan Musial, the pride of Donora, Pa., burst onto the scene with 20 hits in 47 at-bats as a late-season call-up in 1941. Cardinals General Manager Branch Rickey was so impressed that he tore up Musial's contract and increased his salary from $400 to $700 a month.

Musial proved to be a wise investment at any price. He hit .315 as a rookie and made the final putout in the victory that clinched the pennant for St. Louis. He was primarily a gap hitter as a young player — Musial homered just 10 times as a rookie — but after failing to crack 20 homers in his first five seasons, he made a quantum leap to 39 longballs at age 27.

"He figured out that the singles hitters drove Fords and the home run hitters drove Cadillacs," said Hall-of-Fame catcher Al Lopez, who played against Musial as a member of the Pittsburgh Pirates in the 1940s.

The story goes that Musial received his designation as the "The Man" during a road trip to New York, where he routinely wore out the pitching staffs for the Giants and Dodgers.

"He was nicknamed by the Brooklyn fans," said *New York Times* columnist George Vecsey, author of *Stan Musial: An American Life*. "They loved how joyful he was. Musial would hit a ball into the corner and slide into second in a cloud of dust and come up smiling."

Musial's fantastic rookie campaign previewed things to come; he went on to win three MVP Awards and make the NL All-Star team 20 times.

SUCCESS IS FLEETING

Johnny Beazley lived a dream as a young pitcher with the St. Louis Cardinals in the summer of 1942, but barely stuck around long enough to fully enjoy the experience.

Beazley, a product of Nashville, Tenn., cracked the Cardinals' Opening Day roster and quickly established himself as a force in Manager Billy Southworth's rotation. He posted a 21-6 record with a 2.13 ERA, and teamed with Mort Cooper to lead the Cardinals to 106 victories and a National League pennant.

Beazley was equally impressive in October, pitching two complete games against the Yankees in the World Series, including a 4-2 victory in the climactic Game 5 in the Bronx.

But military service beckoned, and Beazley suffered an arm injury when he refused to take it easy during an exhibition game in Memphis while serving in the Army.

"He tried to beat us, I guess," said Cardinals shortstop Marty Marion, who was playing for the opposing team. "He babied it for a couple of years, and it never did come back."

When Beazley returned from the service in 1946, he wasn't the same pitcher. He won just nine more Big League games, and threw his final pitch with the Boston Braves in 1949, going down in history as the quintessential one-year wonder.

Several decades later, Beazley's son, John Jr., told a reporter that his father's demanding workload as a pitcher in the Army was ultimately too much for him to handle.

"They overworked him because he was a star," John Jr. said. "All those generals wanted to see him pitch."

PESKY HITTER

Ted Williams had a way of monopolizing the conversation when he walked into a room, but his domineering presence served to bring out the best in a young shortstop named Johnny Pesky.

In the spring of 1942, Pesky was competing with fellow Minor Leaguer Eddie Pellagrini for a job with the Boston Red Sox. He was having lunch with second baseman Bobby Doerr when Williams strolled into the restaurant and pulled up a chair.

At one point Williams told Pesky, "If you can hit .280, you can help us."

Pesky was dumbfounded by the comment. "What … .280?" he replied. "I can *bunt* that."

THE PESKY POLE

Fenway Park is filled with nooks, crannies and strange quirks, one of which is The Pesky Pole down the right-field line. Nothing screams louder for left-handed hitters to pull the ball down the line and take advantage of the short, 300-foot porch that is seemingly a stone's throw away.

Johnny Pesky became linked with that pole thanks to teammate Mel Parnell, who dubbed it "The Pesky Pole" after Pesky won a game with a bloop hit down the right-field corner.

The nickname gained more traction after Parnell became a Red Sox broadcaster and the term began to pick up more recognition, forever connecting Pesky with the right-field foul pole at Fenway.

Pesky, who had hit .325 the previous season with Triple-A Louisville, proved he was more than just talk. He finished second to Williams in the AL batting race with a .331 average, and led the league with 205 hits and 22 sacrifice bunts. In recognition of his contribution, the baseball writers voted him third in the Most Valuable Player Award balloting behind Williams and Joe Gordon, who took home the prize.

It was no fluke, either. Pesky missed the next three seasons due to military service, but returned to lead the AL in hits in both 1946 and 1947. He teamed with Doerr to give the Red Sox a double-play combination to rival Gordon and Phil Rizzuto in New York.

Beazley's surreal rookie season would be the highlight of a career that ended far too early due to injury.

AMAZING ROOKIE SEASONS

Backing up his confident talk with stellar play on the field, Pesky quickly became one of the best players in the game during his rookie season.

Several decades later, Pesky recalled that Williams seemed impressed by his feistiness in their initial conversation.

"Ted always did like guys who had a little confidence," Pesky said.

PHAN-FAVORITE

IT'S A LONG way from the cornfields of Nebraska to the streets of Philadelphia, but Richie Ashburn made the journey seem easy with his blinding speed, competiveness and good-natured approach, which touched the hearts of hard-bitten Phillies fans.

Ashburn, the pride of Tilden, Neb., spent his youth working in his father's blacksmith shop. The Cleveland Indians and Chicago Cubs tried to sign him to contracts during his teenage years, but both deals were voided because of age restrictions and other technicalities, paving the way for Ashburn to join the Phillies organization in 1945.

After a two-year apprenticeship with the Utica Blue Sox in the Eastern League, Ashburn burst onto the scene with the Big League club in 1948. He received an opportunity to play during Spring Training when incumbent batting champion Harry Walker held out for a more lucrative contract and veteran Charlie Gilbert suffered an ankle injury. Ashburn won the starting center field job and went on to hit a whopping .333 with a National League–leading 32 stolen bases to finish third in voting for the Rookie of the Year Award. Two years later, Ashburn, Robin Roberts, Del Ennis and the rest of Philadelphia's "Whiz Kids" won the National League pennant.

Ashburn's teammates and the Philly fans called him "Whitey" because of his light blond hair, and Ted Williams was credited with nicknaming him "Putt-Putt" because Ashburn ran like he had "twin motors in his pants."

Ashburn played 12 of his 15 Big League seasons in Philadelphia and made the Hall of Fame in 1995. He was a popular broadcaster with the club until he died from a heart attack at age 70. Phillies fans showed up in droves in September 1997 to say goodbye to one of the city's all-time favorites.

> WILLIAMS WAS CREDITED WITH NICKNAMING ASHBURN "PUTT-PUTT" BECAUSE HE RAN LIKE HE HAD "TWIN MOTORS IN HIS PANTS."

TOO MUCH TOO SOON

DICK WAKEFIELD PLAYED to great acclaim as one of baseball's early "bonus babies" with the Detroit Tigers in the early 1940s. His promise was unlimited, but his impact on the field was all too fleeting.

The Tigers paid the extraordinarily high price of $52,000 to sign Wakefield off the University of Michigan campus in June 1941. They even sweetened the deal with a new Cadillac, but Wakefield seemed worth the expense. He looked good in uniform at 6 foot 4, 210 pounds, and the scouts sized him up and saw an outfielder with all the requisite tools for a successful career.

Wakefield, just 22 years old, appeared to be on his way to stardom when he batted .316 with an American League–leading 200 hits and 38 doubles for Detroit in 1943. Some sportswriters looked at his sweet left-handed stroke and made comparisons to Ted Williams. But Wakefield had a questionable work ethic and earned a reputation for flaunting his money.

The well-liked Ashburn endeared himself to his teammates and Philly fans with a combination of talent and a kind personality.

AMAZING ROOKIE SEASONS

A promising outfielder, Wakefield lived up to the hype during his rookie season before eventually flaming out at age 31.

"Most of the resentment came from the newspapers," Wakefield said years later. "Fifty-two thousand was a sockful of money in 1941, and the papers made a big deal of it. They were writing about me every day."

Wakefield's fame didn't last long. After hitting .355 in a half-season with Detroit in 1944, Wakefield entered the Navy and spent the entire 1945 season serving in the Pacific. He was a different player upon his return, hitting a combined .268 for the Tigers from 1946–49. Wakefield drifted to the Yankees, then the Giants, and played his final season in 1952 at the age of 31.

HOME NOT-SO-SWEET HOME

Del Ennis realized every hometown boy's dream when the Phillies signed him as an amateur free agent in 1943. Three years later, at just 21 years of age, the Philadelphia native hit .313 with 17 home runs and 73 RBI, making the All-Star team as Manager Ben Chapman's starting left fielder.

Ennis should have been wildly popular playing in his own backyard, but the converse actually happened. Ennis hit 259 home runs over 11 seasons with the Phillies. But when his tenure in Philadelphia was dissected in hindsight, everyone from the sportswriters to his teammates to Ennis's family members focused on a single question: Why did the locals boo him so much?

For reasons few could understand, Ennis was a constant target for abuse from the Shibe Park faithful. Some fans allegedly booed him for his clumsy outfield play, and others rode him for striking out too much — even though he never whiffed more than 65 times in a season. Ennis's detractors also criticized him for not playing hard, even though he was known for his ferocious double-play takeout slides.

"He was from North Philly, and South Philly didn't like North Philly," Hall-of-Fame right-hander Robin Roberts speculated in a 2009 interview. "He was a big slugger. People talk about how Philly fans are tough on their players. He's the only guy that I played with who they were tough on. They didn't boo any of the rest of us."

> "Ennis was the only guy I played with who fans were tough on. They didn't boo any of the rest of us." — Robin Roberts

CENTERED IN

Manager Mel Ott's New York Giants team was set at two outfield spots in 1947, with Sid Gordon in left field and Willard Marshall in right. The third piece of the puzzle fell into place in Spring Training, when rookie Bobby Thomson won the starting job in center field. Thomson validated the positive first impressions from spring over the next six months, hitting a solid .283 with 29 homers, 85 RBI and 105 runs scored.

In most seasons, that kind of production would have made Thomson a prime candidate for the Rookie of the Year Award, but Thomson happened to pick the wrong season for a coming-out party.

Along with Giants pitcher Larry Jansen — who went 21-5 with a 3.16 ERA in the 1947 campaign — Thomson was overshadowed by Jackie Robinson, who broke the color barrier with the Brooklyn Dodgers that season while hitting .297 with 29 stolen bases.

Despite his solid performance on the field, Philly fans gave the native Ennis a hard time from the stands.

Thomson, a native of Glasgow, Scotland, moved to Staten Island, N.Y., with his family at age 2 and went by the nickname "The Staten Island Scot." He hit 264 home runs in a 15-year career with the Giants and four other clubs, and earned enduring fame with a single, timely swing late in the 1951 season. Thomson's playoff home run against Ralph Branca at the Polo Grounds capped off a miraculous comeback to win the pennant for the Giants, and would forever be known as the "Shot Heard 'Round the World."

A MEMORABLE SHOT

In his rookie year, Bobby Thomson proved that he was blossoming into a Major League star for years to come, but there was still no way to know that four years later, he would hit arguably the most famous home run in Big League history.

In 1951, the Giants had been trailing the Dodgers by a seemingly insurmountable 13 games in August. But they battled back and forced a tie for first place and a best-of-three playoff series between the two teams for the pennant.

With the Giants trailing, 4-1, heading into the ninth inning of the decisive Game 3, the situation looked bleak. New York refused to throw in the towel, though. After the Giants plated one run, the Dodgers replaced starter Don Newcombe with Ralph Branca to face Thomson with two runners on base.

Thomson then forever etched his name in Major League annals. He drove a pitch deep to left field that just cleared the wall at the Polo Grounds, winning the game and sending the crowd into a frenzy. Making his now-famous call, Giants broadcaster Russ Hodges exclaimed, "The Giants win the pennant! The Giants win the pennant!"

NERVES OF STEEL

LEFT-HANDED PITCHER Gene Bearden experienced a season for the ages with the 1948 Indians. He rode his knuckleball to 20 victories, beat Boston in a one-game playoff to clinch the pennant for Cleveland, and picked up a win and a save as the Indians outlasted the Boston Braves in the World Series.

It appeared his future was bright, but Bearden would ultimately be mentioned in the same breath with such forgettables as Bob Grim, Bill Voiselle, Johnny Beazley and Cliff Melton as pitchers who won 20 games in their first full Big League season, but never came close to matching that tally again.

Bearden got a late start in the Big Leagues because of World War II. He was a machinist's mate aboard USS Helena in the South Pacific in 1943 when the ship sank after being hit by Japanese torpedoes. Bearden suffered head wounds and a knee injury and drifted for three days on a life raft before being rescued.

After Bearden's breakthrough regular season in 1948, Cleveland Manager Lou Boudreau shocked experts by picking him over future Hall of Famers Bob Feller and Bob Lemon to start a one-game playoff against the Boston Red Sox. Bearden pitched a complete-game five-hitter in an 8-3 Cleveland rout and tacked on 10.2 scoreless innings in the World Series.

But once the scouting report made the rounds and hitters learned to lay off the knuckleball early in the count, Bearden was never the same. He pitched his final Big League season in 1953 and retired with a 45-38 career record in the Majors.

SIZING HIM UP

AT 6-4, 220 pounds, Don Newcombe was an imposing presence when he walked into a room. As National League hitters could attest, Newcombe was equally foreboding standing on a pitcher's mound.

In 1949, Newcombe followed Jackie Robinson, Dan Bankhead and Roy Campanella as the fourth African-American to appear for the Brooklyn Dodgers. He posted a 17-8 record

Bearden displayed intestinal fortitude that was rare for a rookie, winning a one-game playoff and holding the Braves scoreless in the World Series.

with a 3.17 ERA, and hit .229 in 96 at-bats to establish himself as a budding double threat. At age 23, Newcombe made the All-Star team and won Rookie of the Year. Then, he played admirably in two Series starts, only to suffer 1-0 and 6-4 losses to the New York Yankees.

"Newk" was plagued by his fair share of demons. Although he went on to win 149 games in 10 Major League seasons, he had a tough time shaking the label of "underachiever." Newcombe was angered by the perception among reporters that he was something less than a "big-game pitcher," and he had a fear of flying that was so pronounced, he visited a hypnotist in hopes of an unorthodox cure. On top of all of that, he developed an alcohol problem that gradually took a toll on his career.

"In 1956, I was the best pitcher in baseball," Newcombe said. "Four years later, I was out of the Major Leagues. It must have been the drinking. When you're young, you can handle it, but the older you get, the more it bothers you."

Once his playing career ended, Newcombe channeled his personal experiences into helping others. He spent years as a counselor, helping fellow athletes avoid the pitfalls of alcohol and substance abuse.

> NEWCOMBE FOLLOWED ROBINSON, BANKHEAD AND CAMPANELLA AS THE FOURTH AFRICAN-AMERICAN TO APPEAR FOR THE DODGERS. AT 23, HE MADE THE ALL-STAR TEAM AND WON ROOKIE OF THE YEAR.

FOREVER YOUNG

SATCHEL PAIGE CELEBRATED his 42nd birthday on July 7, 1948 — the same day Cleveland Owner Bill Veeck signed him to a contract that made him the American League's first African-American pitcher. It was an incredible thrill for Paige, a former baseball legend in the Negro Leagues, but not all the reaction was positive. Some prominent voices in the press dismissed the signing as just a gimmick.

"Veeck has gone too far in his quest of publicity," J.G. Taylor Spink wrote in the *Sporting News*. "To sign a hurler at Paige's age is to demean the standards of baseball in the big circuits."

Fans around the league were too busy enjoying the show to express any moral outrage. Paige debuted in relief against the St. Louis Browns and treated a crowd of 34,780 at Municipal Stadium to an assortment of offerings from various arm angles and wind-ups.

"Satchel didn't mow 'em down, but he kept them swinging," wrote the *Cleveland Plain Dealer*. "With a carload of different pitches, he showed 'em how it's done in as grand a coming-out party as any ballplayer ever had."

Word spread quickly, and Paige attracted a total of 201,829 fans in his first three starts. He went 6-1 with a 2.48 ERA in 21 appearances, and the baseball writers had to give him serious consideration when they filled out their Rookie of the Year ballots. Paige joked that he would have been forced to turn down the award if so honored.

"I wasn't sure what year the gentlemen had in mind," he said.

His 42 years of age notwithstanding, Paige turned in a fine "rookie" season in 1948.

CHAPTER 8
SACRIFICE

One after another, prominent Major Leaguers in the 1940s embraced their responsibility to their country and left the baseball field behind for life-and-death pursuits. The selfless mindset of the era was personified by Cleveland Indians pitcher Bob Feller, who put a promising career on hold to join the Navy after the Japanese attacked Pearl Harbor. Feller missed three full seasons and most of a fourth because of military service. He would finish his career with 266 victories, but he never regretted falling short of 300. "I wanted to go," he said years later. "I didn't feel it was my duty. I felt it was my right."

PERSPECTIVE

Cy Young and Walter Johnson are the only pitchers in Major League history with more than 400 victories. Warren Spahn, who ranks sixth on the game's career list with 363 wins, might have joined them if not for missing three seasons because of Army service in World War II. But Spahn gained a perspective from his war years that made statistical achievements seem trivial in comparison.

"After what I went through overseas, I never thought of anything I was told to do in baseball as hard work," Spahn said. "You get over that when you spend days on end sleeping in frozen tank tracks in enemy-threatened territory. The Army taught me what's important and what isn't."

Spahn made it to the Majors with the Boston Braves in 1942, but Manager Casey Stengel demoted him to the Minors when Spahn refused to drill Pee Wee Reese in an exhibition game. The following year, Spahn enlisted in the Army, where he amassed an impressive record of service to his country.

Spahn served with the 276th Engineer Combat Battalion in Belgium, and his engineering unit later helped repair the strategically important Ludendorff Bridge in Remagen, Germany,

ALL-TIME WINS LEADERS
1. Cy Young 511
2. Walter Johnson 417
3. Pete Alexander 373
4. Christy Mathewson 373
5. Pud Galvin 365
6. **Warren Spahn 363**
7. Kid Nichols 361
8. Greg Maddux 355
9. Roger Clemens 354
10. Tim Keefe 342

Spahn's 363 career victories are the most all time among left-handed pitchers.

while under heavy fire. Spahn received a battlefield commission to second lieutenant, and returned home with a Purple Heart and a Bronze Star.

Spahn resumed his Big League career at the age of 25 and quickly made up for lost time. He led the Majors with 202 wins during the 1950s and surpassed 20 victories 13 times in his historic career.

BREAK IN THE ACTION

MICKEY VERNON'S REPUTATION as a terrific sportsman and monument to congeniality earned him the nickname "The Gentleman First Baseman." Former President Dwight Eisenhower once called Vernon his favorite player, and Ike wasn't alone in his admiration.

"Mickey Vernon is as silent as a night watchman, as conservative as a banker and as well-behaved as a vicar," one baseball writer observed.

Vernon made seven All-Star teams, won two batting titles and banged out 2,495 hits in a career spanning four decades.

He played three seasons as the first baseman for the Washington Senators before joining the U.S. Navy in late 1943, spending much of his time during the war on Ulithi Atoll, a small island south of Guam. The area wasn't big enough to accommodate a baseball field, so Vernon and his fellow sailors played softball instead.

The time away didn't hurt Vernon's swing. He returned to Washington in 1946 and hit a league-leading .353 with 51 doubles. Back problems early in his career put a crimp in Vernon's production, but he became a more consistent hitter after surgery to remove his appendix in 1949.

Vernon remained a popular figure in baseball long after his retirement in 1960. In 2003, the residents of his hometown of Marcus Hook, Pa., dedicated a bronze statue in his honor in the town square. "They didn't tell me about it because they knew I'd try to talk them out of it," Vernon said.

> "MICKEY VERNON IS AS SILENT AS A NIGHT WATCHMAN, AS CONSERVATIVE AS A BANKER, AND AS WELL-BEHAVED AS A VICAR."

UNSTOPPABLE

BERT SHEPARD MADE his only appearance in a Major League Baseball box score on Aug. 4, 1945, in a 15-4 Boston Red Sox victory over the Washington Senators at Griffith Park. His stat line doesn't do justice to the pain he endured or the obstacles he overcame to enjoy his moment in the sun.

Shepard, an Indiana native, plugged away in the Minors with middling success until 1942, when he enlisted in the Army during World War II. Two years later, he was piloting a P-38 when his aircraft was shot down on a mission, about 70 miles from Berlin. When Shepard awoke four days later and in a Nazi hospital, his head was wrapped in bandages and his right leg had been amputated. While his baseball career was immediately threatened, more precariously Shepard's life hung in the balance behind enemy lines.

Luckily, Shepard had fate on his side. An Austrian doctor named Ladislaus Loidl intervened to save his life, and Shepard was released in 1945 as part of a prisoner exchange. He was fitted with an artificial leg at Walter Reed Hospital upon his return home, and a meeting

Had he not lost two seasons to military duty, Vernon might have hit 500 career doubles and 200 home runs.

with Under Secretary of War Robert Patterson paved the way for an invitation to Senators camp in Spring Training.

Shepard signed with Washington in 1945 and appeared against Brooklyn in a July exhibition game to sell war bonds. A month later, he experienced the real thing. With the Senators down 12 runs to Boston, Manager Ossie Bluege summoned Shepard to the mound. Shepard struck out George "Catfish" Metkovich to escape a bases loaded jam, and allowed only one run over 5.1 innings. He finished his Big League career with a 1.69 ERA.

NO FLUKE

Cecil Travis's Major League debut heralded great things. He walked into the Washington Senators' clubhouse as a scared, 19-year-old injury fill-in, and walked off the field as a record-setter.

Travis, summoned from Chattanooga of the Southern Association to replace injured veteran Ossie Bluege, put on a show in an 11-10 win over Cleveland on May 16, 1933. He singled in his first five plate appearances to join Fred Clarke of the 1894 Louisville Colonels as just the second player to collect five hits in his first game.

Travis was no fluke. Over the next seven seasons, he proceeded to hit .319, .318, .317, .344, .335, .292 and .322, and Ted Williams, the ultimate authority on hitting, called him "one of the five best left-handed hitters I ever saw."

If Travis was overlooked, it was because he spent so much time in the shadow of baseball's elite bats. In 1941, Travis batted .359 and led the American League with 218 hits. But Williams batted .406 and Joe DiMaggio hit safely in 56 straight games, so his wondrous season fell through the cracks.

Ultimately, Travis lacked the requisite amount of staying power. He missed almost four seasons because of military service during World War II and suffered two frozen toes in the Battle of the Bulge. When Travis returned from the battlefield in 1946, he was surprised to find that his skills as a hitter had waned. His bat speed and timing were irretrievably gone.

"All I know is that pitches I used to hit the fool out of were getting me out," Travis said in a 1991 interview. "I figured it was time to go back where I came from: the farm."

Travis returned home to the family farm in Georgia, where he lived until his death in 1993. Even if his time in the Majors had not been interrupted by service, it's unclear if Travis would have been elected to the Hall of Fame. Nevertheless, some baseball writers have called him the most talented player never to receive a Hall of Fame vote.

LEGENDARY ABSENCE

Joe DiMaggio's war service occurred far from the battlefields of Europe and Asia, where many of his peers risked their lives in combat and hazardous support duty, but time away from home still took a physical and emotional toll on the "Yankee Clipper."

DiMaggio, 28 years old and fresh off his seventh straight All-Star season with the Yankees, enlisted in the Army in early 1943 and was assigned to an air base in Santa Ana, Calif. He served as a physical training instructor and, naturally, played center field on the squad's baseball team.

The following year, he was transferred to Hawaii, where he fell victim to stress and nearly constant stomach problems. DiMaggio's first marriage was unraveling, and he felt wronged that his career had been interrupted by the war. "There wasn't anyone else in that unit who hated this war like DiMaggio," wrote author Richard Ben Cramer in the book, *Joe DiMaggio: The Hero's Life*.

Travis sported a .327 career average through 1941, placing among the AL's top five hitters three times.

DiMaggio returned to New York in 1946 and played six more seasons until his retirement in 1951. He hit .290 with 25 homers in his first season back, and would blast a total of 142 longballs after his tour of duty was up. But his career numbers — 361 home runs and 2,214 hits — clearly suffered from his hiatus in the military. DiMaggio became the ultimate case of what could have been, even though his career as it stood was enough to gain election to Cooperstown.

"Though he never came within a thousand miles of actual combat, DiMaggio resented the war with an intensity equal to the most battle-scarred private," wrote biographer David Jones. "It had robbed him of the best years of his career … Those three years, 1943–45, would carve a gaping hole in DiMaggio's career totals, creating an absence that would be felt like a missing limb."

WHAT MIGHT HAVE BEEN …

TED WILLIAMS SPENT 19 years setting records, winning awards and laying waste to American League pitching, but he also spent five years in the Marines, first as a flight instructor during World War II and later as a fighter pilot in Korea. Without the time away from the game, Williams likely would have surpassed 3,000 hits and might have approached 700 home runs, but he refused to classify himself as a hero or dwell on the numbers he might have had.

"That time in the service is something you can never duplicate or match," Williams said in a 1997 interview. "And you're damn lucky if you come out of it in one hunk."

Williams' introduction to military service came against a backdrop of scrutiny in Boston and beyond. Williams initially received a deferment as the sole provider for his mother, May, who was separated from his father and worked for the Salvation Army. But his resolve began to weaken when Tigers catcher Mickey Cochrane gave Williams a personal tour of the Great Lakes Naval Training Center, and he enlisted in the Navy in the spring of 1942. Two years later, he was commissioned a second lieutenant in the Marines.

> "THAT TIME IN THE SERVICE IS SOMETHING YOU CAN NEVER DUPLICATE OR MATCH. AND YOU'RE DAMN LUCKY IF YOU COME OUT OF IT IN ONE HUNK." TED WILLIAMS

Williams' 20-10 vision, superb hand-eye coordination and natural swagger were ideal for a pilot, and he spent most of World War II as a flight instructor. He was bound for combat in the Pacific when fighting ceased and he was able to resume his baseball career with the Red Sox. In the six seasons following his return, Williams managed to keep posting incredible numbers; a .340 average, .485 on-base percentage, 196 home runs and 832 walks to just 246 strikeouts from 1946–51 further cemented Williams' legendary status, even with three seasons missing from his early prime.

His time away from the military wouldn't be long, as Williams returned to the Marines at age 33 and flew 39 combat missions in Korea. He survived a near-death experience when his F-9 Panther was hit by anti-aircraft fire and crash-landed in a field near Pyongyang. Williams, like Joe DiMaggio, carries an air of "what if" about his numbers. But, if nothing else, the five years Williams dedicated to military service only serve to bolster his legend as a true American icon.

Williams won four of his six batting titles following his first return from the military, including a .388 mark in 1957.

CHAPTER 9
CHARACTERS AND CONTROVERSY

Long before a black cat passed in front of the Cubs' dugout in 1969 and a die-hard fan named Steve Bartman earned a place in infamy by trying to catch a foul ball in 2003, this franchise's fate was sealed with a bizarre encounter at the 1945 World Series. Or was it? Chicago tavern owner Bill Sianis brought his pet goat to a Series game between the Cubs and Detroit Tigers at Wrigley Field, and allegedly put a jinx on the hometown team when asked to leave the premises. The factual details remain hazy decades later, but good luck telling a Cubs fan that the Billy Goat Curse is fiction.

COMIC RELIEF

MAX PATKIN NEVER planned to be a baseball clown. His first goal was to pitch in the Big Leagues, but a chance encounter with Joe DiMaggio in 1944 sent his career hurtling in a new and unexpected direction.

Patkin, an obscure Minor League pitcher in the Chicago White Sox organization, came face-to-face with his destiny while facing the Yankee Clipper in a military service exhibition game in Hawaii. DiMaggio drove a pitch over the fence into the Pacific Ocean and embarked upon his home run trot while accompanied by Patkin, who had dropped his glove and begun circling the infield in mock disgust.

The crowd loved it, and Patkin's new course was set. In 1946, after a brief fling with Cleveland's Wilkes-Barre farm club in the Eastern League, Patkin called it quits as a player and succeeded Al Schacht as the "Clown Prince of Baseball."

Patkin, blessed with a rubbery face, enormous nose, toothless grin and lanky physique fit for comedy, entertained generations of fans with his corny jokes and slapstick antics until his retirement in 1995. He played an estimated 4,000 ballpark dates over a five-decade span, and appeared as himself in the hit movie *Bull Durham*. Patkin was 79 years old when he died of an aneurysm at his Paoli, Pa., home in 1999.

"I think it's a God-given thing, something that was in me. I was very loose-jointed," Patkin said in a 1989 interview. "I've enjoyed making people laugh. It's been fun. If you can make people laugh, it's an accomplishment."

Patkin's imitation of DiMaggio circling the bases led to a career of entertaining crowds at Minor League ballparks all over the country.

GREAT EXPECTATIONS

CLINT HARTUNG HAD nowhere to go but down when sportswriters hailed him as a combination of Babe Ruth *and* Walter Johnson before he had logged his first at-bat or inning pitched in the Major Leagues. In the end, the New York Giants would have been happy with a reasonable facsimile of Babe Herman or Bucky Walters.

Hartung, nicknamed the "Hondo Hurricane" after his hometown of Hondo, Texas, will forever be remembered as a hyped prospect who failed to perform to expectations. Much of the buildup was attributed to Giants publicist Garry Schumacher, who resorted to some grand hyperbole to sell the New York press on Hartung's potential and sell some tickets at the Polo Grounds.

"He's a sucker if he ever shows up," Schumacher told *The New York Times* before Hartung's arrival. "He should go straight to the Hall of Fame at Cooperstown."

Hartung led his high school team to a state title and burnished his credentials with some amazing statistics against inferior competition in military ball in Hawaii. As a 6-foot-5, 210-pound power hitter and fastball pitcher, he was billed as a classic two-way threat.

But Hartung's impact in New York was minimal. He posted a 29-29 record with a 5.02 ERA as a pitcher and hit .238 with 14 home runs in 378 at-bats over six seasons, and the Giants finally cut their ties with him in 1954.

Hartung's most memorable career moment came as a footnote. He pinch-ran for Don Mueller in the third game of the 1951 playoffs against Brooklyn, eventually coming around to score on Bobby Thomson's "Shot Heard 'Round the World" home run off Ralph Branca.

BROTHERLY GLOVE

THE TOWN OF Atherton, Mo., made a double-barreled contribution to some of the powerhouse St. Louis Cardinals teams of the 1940s.

Mort Cooper, a 6-foot-2, 210-pound right-handed pitcher, posted a 65-22 record for three straight pennant winners from 1942–44. He did it while throwing primarily to his brother, Walker, a three-time All-Star in St. Louis before Branch Rickey sold him to the New York Giants for $175,000 in 1946. The Coopers will be remembered as one of baseball's premier brother battery combinations, along with Wes and Rick Ferrell of the Boston Red Sox and Johnny and Elmer Riddle of the Cincinnati Reds.

Walker was a renowned practical joker, with a fondness for dispensing hot feet and nailing teammates' shoes to the floor. At a beefy 6 foot 3, 210 pounds, he was bestowed with such nicknames as "Hog Jaws" and "Sow Belly."

Mort Cooper pitched his final game in 1949 and died of a lung condition nine years later at age 45. Walker made his final appearance in uniform with the Cardinals in 1957. After his daughter married St. Louis second baseman Don Blasingame, Walker observed, "It's time to quit when you've got a daughter old enough to marry a teammate."

Walker Cooper never made more than $30,000 in the Big Leagues, and in his later years he frequently lamented his meager compensation as a player. "Hell, if Gary Carter is worth $2 million, I'd damn well be worth $2 million," he said in 1990, one year before his death.

Hartung had promise but was held to near-impossible standards even before entering the Major Leagues.

SIBLING RIVALRY

	YRS	W-L	ERA	IP	CG	H	K
Mort Cooper	1938–47, '49	128-75	2.97	1,840.2	128	1,666	913

	YRS	AVG	OBP	SLG	HR	RBI	R
Walker Cooper	1940–57	.285	.332	.464	173	812	573

Brothers Mort (far left) and Walker Cooper shared Major League battery-mates with the St. Louis Cardinals.

CHARACTERS AND CONTROVERSY

CURSED

RED SOX OWNER Harry Frazee allegedly paved the way for decades of torment in Boston with some bad judgment and a non-descript Broadway show. In December 1919, Frazee sold slugger Babe Ruth to the Yankees to finance the production of his play *No No Nanette*. Ruth went on to hit 714 home runs, and Boston fell victim to the Curse of the Bambino.

An equally strange confluence of circumstances helped create some bad karma on the North Side of Chicago. The perceived hex, which extended through the 21st century's first decade, would become known as the "Curse of the Billy Goat."

In the 1930s and '40s, a Greek immigrant named Bill Sianis ran an establishment called the Lincoln Tavern on West Madison Street in Chicago. Sianis would promote his bar with the help of his pet goat, Sonovia, who mingled with customers and once appeared at the *Chicago Tribune* offices during World War II wearing a sign that said, "Buy Defense Bonds."

When the Cubs advanced to the 1945 World Series against Detroit, Sianis bought two tickets to Game 4, one for himself and one for the goat. But when Sonovia began annoying fans in the box seats with his rank odor and bad behavior, Sianis was escorted from the park. After Chicago lost the Series, Sianis sent Cubs Owner Philip Wrigley a telegram with the message, "Who stinks now?"

There was no mention at the time, or in subsequent decades, of a true billy goat "curse." But like the Babe Ruth story, the goat legend gained currency until it became an accepted piece of Cubs lore.

"The notion of a 'billy goat'–inspired hex or curse was a later product of the press, and Sianis was savvy enough to play along with it," wrote historians Richard Johnson and Glenn Stout. Sianis renamed his bar the Billy Goat Tavern and moved it to Michigan Avenue, and the story made for very good business.

CHILD'S PLAY

LOU BOUDREAU MAJORED in physical education at the University of Illinois and played for the Illini basketball team before beginning his professional baseball career. At the tender age of 24, he mailed a letter to Cleveland Indians Owner Alva Bradley suggesting those attributes qualified him to be the team's player-manager.

Boudreau regretted his actions from the moment he dropped the letter in the box. "I look back and realize it was a very brash thing for me to do," he said more than 50 years later. But Bradley was sufficiently intrigued to invite Boudreau to a meeting of club directors. Even more shockingly, the Indians actually picked Boudreau over two other candidates to succeed Roger Peckinpaugh as the team's manager in 1942.

The press immediately dubbed Boudreau the "Boy Manager," but nobody cut him any slack because of his youth. The overall reaction was skeptical, to put it mildly.

"Great! The Indians get a Baby Snooks for a manager and ruin the best shortstop in baseball," wrote one Cleveland reporter. Another editorial said a complaint should be filed against the Indians with the Society for the Prevention of Cruelty to Children.

LOU BOUDREAU'S CAREER STATS AS A PLAYER AND MANAGER

	Seasons	Games	AB	AVG	OBP	HR	RBI	SB	RUNS
Player	15	1,646	6,029	.295	.380	68	789	51	861

	Seasons	Games	Wins	Losses	W-L Pct.	Pennants	WS Titles
Manager	16	2,404	1,162	1,224	.487	1	1

Boudreau's moxie paid off when the Indians accepted the phys ed major's offer to serve as Cleveland's player-manager.

CHARACTERS AND CONTROVERSY

With experience and time, Boudreau proved adept at multi-tasking. In 1948, he won the American League MVP Award and managed the Indians to 97 victories, an AL pennant and a World Series victory over the Boston Braves. At 30 years old, he had reached the pinnacle of his profession, in more ways than one.

GAME OVER

WILLIAM COX BARELY registers in the game's historical timeline. But he committed an egregious sin in the eyes of the baseball establishment, and paid the price in 1943.

Cox, owner of the Philadelphia Phillies, received a lifetime ban from Commissioner Kenesaw Mountain Landis for betting on his team. He was forced to sell his interests to Ruly Carpenter Jr., ending a brief and stormy tenure with the club.

A Yale product who made his money in the lumber business, Cox bought the Phillies for a bargain price during a period of financial distress for the franchise. Phillies historian Rich Westcott described Cox as "a glib and convincing non-stop talker with the promotional instincts of a circus barker." It didn't take long for Cox to alienate the team's board of directors and veteran Manager Bucky Harris with his meddling and impulsive decisions.

With the Phillies playing a series in St. Louis against the Cardinals in May 1943, Cox held a press conference in Philadelphia to announce that he was firing Harris. An irate Harris gathered reporters at his hotel room and said, "He's a fine one to fire me when he gambles on games his club plays."

A subsequent investigation found that Cox had made about 15 to 20 bets of $25 to $100 each on the Phillies to win. Cox contended that the bets were "sentimental" in nature and that he was unaware of baseball's prohibition against gambling, but it ultimately wasn't enough to save his job.

GOOD CALLS

BASEBALL FANS IN New York had the best of both worlds when they turned on the radio and listened to a game during the 1940s. The talent in the broadcast booth was as stellar as the array of talent on the field.

From 1939–53, Brooklyn Dodgers fans had the pleasure of listening to Walter Lanier "Red" Barber, a Mississippi native who made a seamless transition to the big city to call games. "All I did was speak correctly and try not to get my tenses fouled up," Barber said.

"IN A SPORT BUILT FOR RADIO, ALLEN WAS A MASTER DESIGNER." *NEWSDAY*

While Brooklyn General Manager Branch Rickey went to great lengths to prep Jackie Robinson for baseball's integration, he also made sure Barber was in the loop. As one of the game's most prominent voices, Barber was an important conduit to the fan base and a natural opinion shaper. He went to great lengths to put aside his boyhood prejudices and racial sentiments and handle Robinson's debut with professionalism and grace.

"It was the hottest microphone any announcer had to face," Barber recalled in a 1988 interview.

Mel Allen, born in Alabama to Russian-Jewish immigrants, became an institution behind the microphone for a quarter century in the Bronx. He broke in with the New York Yankees in 1939 and went on to broadcast 20 World Series, 24 All-Star Games and,

Barber became an institution in Brooklyn, and had the seemingly unenviable task of calling Jackie Robinson's first Major League game.

perhaps most riveting, the Roger Maris–Mickey Mantle home run chase in 1961 during his illustrious career.

Allen coined the nicknames "Joltin' Joe" for DiMaggio, "Scooter" for Phil Rizzuto and "Old Reliable" for Tommy Henrich. He unveiled his catchphrase — "How about that?" — after DiMaggio homered in three straight games after returning from a heel injury in 1949.

"In a sport built by and for radio, Allen was a master designer, the unquestioned voice and conscience of the Yankees," *Newsday* wrote in Allen's obituary in 1996.

WINNING EDGE

BILL VEECK'S TALENTS as an innovator were on display long before he took over Big League teams in Cleveland, St. Louis and Chicago. As the Triple-A Milwaukee Brewers' owner from 1941–45, Veeck hired Charlie Grimm and Casey Stengel to manage, and gave away live squab — a type of pigeon — and 200-pound blocks of ice to lucky fans in offbeat promotions.

Veeck also wasn't above seeking a competitive advantage by any means necessary. With the Brewers short on left-handed power hitters, he installed a 60-foot high chicken-wire fence to make it more challenging for opponents to go deep. He used a hydraulic motor to raise the fence during opposing at-bats, and lower it when the Brewers hit. The American Association quickly responded by outlawing the subterfuge.

"Until they passed the rule, understand, this was all perfectly legal, even if it did not necessarily qualify us for that season's Abner Doubleday Award for sportsmanship above and beyond the call of duty," Veeck wrote in his autobiography.

INNOVATOR

While his most notable move might have been signing the American League's first African-American player in Larry Doby, Bill Veeck's tenure as an owner ensured that the daily grind of the Major League season never became monotonous. After taking over the Cleveland Indians in 1947, Veeck immediately put the games on radio.

As his career went on, Veeck's ideas became more outrageous. One of his most infamous moves was to sign 3-foot-7 Eddie Gaedel when he owned the St. Louis Browns. Gaedel walked in his only Major League plate appearance.

Veeck continued to think outside the box, adding an "exploding scoreboard" at Comiskey Park for whenever the White Sox hit a home run. He also added surnames to the backs of jerseys. When the Cardinals' Curt Flood sued MLB in 1970 over the legality of the reserve clause, Veeck was the only owner to testify in support of Flood and free agency.

In 1976, Veeck decided to sign Minnie Minoso in order to give Minoso the ability to play in four different decades. He did the same in 1980, giving Minoso appearances in five decades. Veeck also helped come up with the idea for Disco Demolition Night, which resulted in riots at Comiskey Park.

Sometimes good, sometimes bad, but always interesting, Bill Veeck cemented his legacy as one of the great owners.

FIGHTING WORDS

JOE MEDWICK COMPILED an impressive record of achievement in 17 seasons with the Cardinals and three other clubs. He made 10 All-Star teams and hit .374 with 31 homers and 154 RBI in 1937 to win a Triple Crown. It remained the last NL Triple Crown of the century.

His "Gashouse Gang" teammates referred to Medwick as "Ducky" for his distinctive, sauntering walk, but Medwick himself was partial to the nickname "Muscles." At a compact 5 foot 10, 185 pounds, he had a reputation for being pugnacious and never backing down from fights — against teammates and opponents alike.

"That Medwick don't fight fair," former teammate Dizzy Dean once observed. "He whoops you before you can say a word."

Medwick's toughness was both a blessing and a curse.

That capacity for confrontation bought Medwick more trouble than he anticipated during the 1940 season.

Just a few days after the Cardinals traded him to Brooklyn in June, Medwick exchanged words with former St. Louis teammate Bob Bowman during an elevator ride in the New Yorker hotel in Manhattan. Dodgers Manager Leo Durocher, who was also in the elevator, recalled Bowman saying, "I'll take care of both of you guys. Wait and see."

Bowman was true to his word. After giving up several line drive hits, Bowman beaned Medwick in the head, precipitating a near-riot at Ebbets Field. Medwick would play eight more seasons, but his days as a perennial batting title contender had come and gone. "Medwick never again was quite the same savage badball hitter of the past," wrote Bob Broeg of the *St. Louis Post–Dispatch*.

ROBBED

TED WILLIAMS HAD a frosty relationship with Boston Red Sox fans, as evidenced by a celebrated spitting incident and his refusal to tip his cap to the crowd during his final game at Fenway Park in 1960. But it paled in contrast to his clashes with sportswriters, whom Williams derisively referred to as the "Knights of the Keyboard."

After one of Williams' most productive seasons, his testy relationship with the press may have helped cost him a Most Valuable Player Award.

One year after winning his first MVP Award, Williams won the Triple Crown in 1947 with a .343 batting average, 32 home runs and 114 RBI, but the MVP this time went to New York's Joe DiMaggio in an extremely close vote. In his autobiography, *My Turn at Bat*, Williams pointed the finger at a single scribe for denying him the honor he felt he deserved.

"It came out that one Boston writer didn't even put me in the top 10 on his ballot," Williams recounted. "A 10th-place vote would have given me two points and the Most Valuable Player Award … the writer's name was Mel Webb."

But other accounts cast doubt on that assertion. In a 1948 story, Harold Kaese of the *Boston Globe* identified Boston's three MVP voters as Red Sox beat writers Joe Cashman, Burt Whitman and Jack Malaney. Kaese later described the anonymous Williams-slighter as a "Midwestern writer who couldn't even see Ted ranked with the top 10!"

The mystery voter was never solved, but Williams eventually enjoyed some vindication. He steamrolled New York's Phil Rizzuto and Joe Page in 1949 for a second MVP Award.

BUSTED 'LIP'

WHILE JACKIE ROBINSON was making history by breaking the color barrier in 1947, Brooklyn Manager Leo "the Lip" Durocher was in California chopping down trees, clearing the ground for a new house, and uttering curses under his breath at Commissioner Happy Chandler, the man responsible for his forced, one-year sabbatical from the game.

Durocher, whose profile extended well beyond the ballfield because of his marriage to actress Laraine Day and friendships with George Raft and other Hollywood figures, landed on Major League Baseball's radar through his associations with gamblers and other "unsavory" characters — including two men named Memphis Engelberg and Connie Immerman. Engelberg, a former bookmaker and skilled horse racing bettor, occasionally gave Durocher tips at the track. Immerman, who had once run the Cotton Club in New York, managed a gambling casino in Havana and was also a casual friend of Durocher's.

Chandler took note in 1947 when reports surfaced that the two gamblers had shown up to watch a Dodgers-Yankees exhibition game in Havana in seats next to the box belonging

Although he should have been a shoo-in for the 1947 MVP Award, Williams believed he lost the honor due to one writer's lack of support.

to Yankees President Larry MacPhail. Chandler fined both clubs $2,000, and suspended Durocher one year for what he later called an "accumulation of sins."

The press came down on Durocher's side, surprisingly as the manager's healthy ego and flair for self-promotion rarely enhanced his popularity.

"Commissioner Chandler had done the seemingly impossible," wrote *Time* Magazine. "He had made Leo Durocher a sympathetic figure."

"I must admit, I didn't think anybody could do that," Chandler said in recounting the incident in 1971.

COURT CASE

Daniel Lewis Gardella's name doesn't typically appear alongside that of Curt Flood, Dave McNally and other baseball labor trailblazers, but he could well be credited with batting leadoff for the cause.

Gardella, a New York native, was an undersized, marginally-talented outfielder who batted .272 and hit 18 home runs with 71 RBI for the New York Giants in 1945 while the talent pool was depleted because of the war. He knew his playing time would diminish with the return of Big League war veterans in 1946, but another opportunity awaited: Sal Maglie, Mickey Owen, Max Lanier and other Major Leaguers were following the money trail to Mexico, and Gardella doubled his $5,000 salary by signing with the Veracruz Azules of the Mexican League.

Commissioner Happy Chandler banned Gardella and more than 20 other Mexican League players from returning to the Majors for five years, and in 1947, Gardella filed a suit in U.S. District Court charging baseball with violating federal antitrust laws. The suit contended that baseball had deprived Gardella of the opportunity to make a living through the reserve clause, which bound a player to his team for the duration of his career unless he was traded or released.

Gardella eventually dropped the suit in exchange for a reported $60,000 settlement. In 1950, he returned for a one-at-bat cameo with the St. Louis Cardinals.

"I sued because I love the game and I wanted to play," Gardella said decades later.

> "I SUED BECAUSE I LOVE THE GAME AND I WANTED TO PLAY." Danny Gardella

WALK-OUT

Joseph Floyd "Arky" Vaughan developed a reputation as a steady producer over 14 Big League seasons. He also personified the notion that actions speak louder than words.

Vaughan, an Arkansas native who grew up in California, achieved the bulk of his fame as an infielder with the Pittsburgh Pirates in the 1930s. The Dodgers acquired him in a multi-player trade in 1941, but Vaughan's tenure in Brooklyn took a bizarre and inexplicable turn during the summer of 1943.

Brooklyn Manager Leo Durocher, never one to coddle players, showered pitcher Bobo Newsom with abuse during an argument over a play that had cost the Dodgers a game. Vaughan took offense, and responded by wrapping his uniform in a bundle, handing it to Durocher, and making it clear he had no interest in playing for him anymore. The Dodgers even threatened to walk out in support of Vaughan before order was restored.

Vaughan returned home to California at the end of the season and took a three-year sabbatical from baseball before rejoining the Dodgers in 1947. Four years after his retirement, Vaughan died in a boating accident at age 40.

Vaughan's children later said that his hiatus from baseball was a product of family obligations, rather than lingering feelings of discontent with Durocher. Vaughan's brother Glenn had gone off to war, and someone needed to run the family farm back home in California. "This Durocher thing, we really feel, is a myth," Vaughan's son Bob said in an interview with the *Los Angeles Times* in 1986.

Gardella was banned from the Bigs after he signed with a team in the Mexican League.

Vaughan (right) walked out on the Dodgers after seeing the verbal abuse that Durocher (far left) laid into his Brooklyn Dodgers teammate.

CHAPTER 10
PENNANT RACES

In 1949, the New York Yankees began an astonishing decade-plus run of success under new manager Casey Stengel. Appropriately enough, the starting point was against their favorite foils from Boston. After an epic pennant race, the Bronx Bombers won the final two regular season games against Boston to advance to the World Series. That began a string of seven world championships and 10 pennants in 12 seasons with Stengel at the helm. The Red Sox, meanwhile, finished second four times in the decade and lost a heartbreaker to the St. Louis Cardinals in the 1946 Series. They were the quintessential bridesmaids, never the brides.

BOSTON BLUES

THE RED SOX finished second in the AL four times in the 1940s — and lost the 1946 World Series to the Cardinals — so baseball fans in Boston were accustomed to disappointment. Just when Red Sox fans didn't think things could get any worse after losing a one-game play-off in 1948, the '49 team once again broke New Englanders' hearts, prolonging the suspense until the final day of the season before coming up short against the rival Yankees.

While injuries limited Joe DiMaggio to just 76 games in 1949, Ted Williams hit .343 with 43 homers and 159 RBI and won his second career MVP Award. As a stirring pennant race neared its conclusion in early October, the Red Sox needed to capture just one of the final two games to send the Yankees home for the winter.

Boston's chances looked good in the penultimate game, when the Sox took an early 4-0 lead behind 25-game winner Mel Parnell. Boston catcher Birdie Tebbetts, feeling his oats, joked to Phil Rizzuto that the Red Sox were planning to start an untested rookie, Yale product Frank Quinn, in the season finale once they had officially clinched the title.

The Yankees, properly inspired, staged a furious rally to win, 5-4, and set up a winner-take-all matchup on the final day of the season.

Boston's Ellis Kinder and New York's Vic Raschi faced off in a monumental pitcher's duel, but the Yankees pulled ahead against the Red Sox bullpen in the eighth inning to win, 5-3, and snatch the pennant from the Red Sox's clutches.

While the Yankees went on to beat Brooklyn in the World Series — a title that touched off a run of five straight titles under Manager Casey Stengel — their rivals from Boston went home and spent a long winter contemplating what might have been.

"It was the longest train ride we've ever had," Parnell said.

The Yankees' 1949 pennant win under Stengel began an unprecedented run of success.

THE ROOKIE VS. RAPID ROBERT

Cleveland's Bob Feller, widely acclaimed as the best pitcher in baseball in 1940, looked like the surest of sure things when he took the mound against Detroit on the final weekend of the season. The Indians needed to sweep a three-game series from the Tigers to win the American League pennant, and Feller would be opposed by a 30-year-old rookie who had been written off as nothing but a sacrificial lamb.

That rookie, Floyd Giebell, didn't leave much of a legacy in the Major Leagues, but he embodies the idea that, on any given day, even the most obscure baseball journeymen are capable of wondrous things.

As the final weekend approached, Detroit Manager Del Baker threw everyone a curve by selecting Giebell to oppose the great Feller and save two of his top starters, Bobo Newsom and Schoolboy Rowe, for the final two games.

Baker's hunch to start the rookie paid dividends when Giebell threw a complete-game six-hitter to beat the indomitable Feller, 2-0, sending the Tigers to the World Series and bringing Cleveland's season to a shockingly premature end. Feller walked a season-high eight batters in the loss.

The Cleveland papers referred to Giebell as "the kid" and "the youngster," even though he was nine years older than Feller, but Giebell didn't pitch like a rookie, He stifled the Cleveland offense and made Rudy York's two-run homer stand up as the difference maker in a complete-game win.

"Even if I make 100 bum guesses before I retire, they can't take this one away from me," Baker said in the Detroit clubhouse after the game. "I had a hunch the kid would deliver, but I never dreamed he would pitch such a perfect game."

GUT CHECK

In 1948, one of the most stirring pennant races in baseball history culminated in a dream scenario, with the Cleveland Indians and Boston Red Sox meeting in a one-game playoff for the right to face the NL champion Boston Braves in the World Series.

Lou Boudreau, Cleveland's 31-year-old player-manager, invited considerable second-guessing with a pair of gutsy calls. He chose rookie knuckleballer Gene Bearden to start on one day's rest, and inserted outfielder Allie Clark at first base, a position Clark had never played, because Boudreau wanted to stack his order with right-handed bats.

Boudreau was fortunate. As Cleveland's starting shortstop, he also had the ability to influence the game with contributions beyond his lineup decisions.

Boudreau went 4 for 4 with a pair of home runs, teammate Ken Keltner added a three-run shot, and the Indians blitzed the Red Sox, 8-3, for the American League pennant. Bearden pitched an effectively wild complete game, walking five while striking out six in picking up his 20th win of the season. The Indians celebrated the victory later in the evening with a raucous team party, during which players alternately threw playful punches and shared emotional embraces.

In hindsight, Boston Manager Joe McCarthy would be assailed for his decision to start journeyman Denny Galehouse over veterans Jack Kramer, Joe Dobson, Ellis Kinder and young left-hander Mel Parnell, who was so convinced he would be pitching that he went to dinner and was home in bed at 9 p.m. the night before the game. Galehouse would last just three innings, surrendering four of Cleveland's eight runs and allowing two home runs in taking a dispiriting loss.

"I was the guy that should have pitched it," Parnell maintained years later. "I had the most rest. I should have been the pitcher of that game, without a doubt."

Bearden was mobbed by his teammates after he pitched a pennant-winning complete game against Boston.

TWIST OF FATE

The 1942 Brooklyn Dodgers roster included an array of brand names and talented ballplayers enjoying very productive seasons. Center fielder Pete Reiser batted .310 and led the National League with 20 stolen bases. First baseman Dolph Camilli was second in the league with 26 home runs and 109 RBI. Left fielder Joe Medwick hit .300 while starter Whit Wyatt won 19 games and swingman Larry French went 15-4 to finish second in the league with a .789 winning percentage.

In the end, all those statistical achievements amounted to little more than heartache and an unenviable distinction: The '42 Dodgers are remembered by many fans as one of the greatest second-place teams in baseball history. They certainly would have preferred to be remembered as the opposite.

Fresh off their first pennant in 21 years, the Dodgers broke out of the gate quickly and took a 10-game lead in early August. Their season peaked on Aug. 5, when Max Macon tossed a two-hit shutout at Ebbets Field to beat the Giants, 4-0, and improve Brooklyn's record to 74-30. The Dodgers seemed relaxed, confident and ready to seal the deal under Manager Leo Durocher.

But the season took a remarkable twist over the next seven weeks. The St. Louis Cardinals staged an amazing 43-8 late-season run to catch and pass the Dodgers, who went 30-20 down the stretch only to find that wasn't good enough. Stan Musial and the Cards won five of their last six meetings with Brooklyn — including three one-run victories — to leave the stunned Dodgers wondering how things could have unraveled so quickly.

NO LEAD TOO SAFE

The Dodgers' blown lead in 1942 was heartbreaking, but it might not have even been the most difficult collapse that Brooklyn fans ever had to stomach. Just nine years later, the 1951 Dodgers held a 12.5-game lead on Aug. 12 over the crosstown rival Giants. During the ensuing weeks, the Giants feverously made up ground, forcing a winner-take-all final game of the season against the Dodgers. After falling behind, 4-1, the Giants rallied for four runs in the ninth, capped by Bobby Thomson's legendary walk-off three-run home run to send the Giants to the World Series.

The Dodgers aren't the only team to endure such heartbreak. The 1964 Phillies blew a 6.5-game lead with 12 to play to the Cardinals. Philadelphia would experience its own historic comeback in 2007, though. Trailing by seven games with 17 to play, it looked like the Phillies' season was just about over. But the Phils caught fire, going 13-4, and the Mets went into a tailspin, posting a 5-12 record. With a chance at a one-game playoff on the line, the Mets' nightmare September came to an end after a loss on the final day of the season to the Marlins.

ALL GROWN UP

If anyone ever needed a reminder why Stan Musial was so respected by teammates and opponents alike, it came during a routine game in Brooklyn on June 23, 1946.

As Musial stepped to the plate against the Dodgers' Joe Hatten, the Ebbets Field crowd began chanting, "Here comes the man!" *St. Louis Post-Dispatch* columnist Bob Broeg couldn't clearly hear the words from his perch high up in the press box, but he learned the specifics later that evening while having dinner with Cardinals traveling secretary Leo Ward. When Broeg recounted the incident in the next day's newspaper, the sobriquet "Stan the Man" was officially born.

Despite a starting infield that included stars (from left) Camilli, Billy Herman, Pee Wee Reese and Arky Vaughan, the '42 Dodgers may always be remembered for a second-place finish.

Dodgers fans, "though crying in their beer, could appreciate excellence even when they saw it in an enemy baseball uniform," Broeg wrote. Musial went 1 for 2 with two walks on the day as the Cardinals won, 4-2.

Musial cemented his reputation as The Man in the second half of the '46 season, hitting .380 with a .633 slugging percentage after the All-Star break to lead St. Louis past Brooklyn for the National League pennant. The Cardinals clinched a World Series spot by defeating the Dodgers in a best-of-three playoff series in early October. Musial had two hits in the two-game sweep and finished 1946 with a league-leading .365 average, a mark that Musial would best just once in the last 17 seasons of his Hall-of-Fame career. Musial's 725 career doubles — 50 of which came in that special 1946 season that birthed his nickname — rank third all-time, one two-bagger ahead of Ty Cobb.

In Spring Training of 1946, Musial had received a five-year, $125,000 offer to play in Mexico, but he declined even though his salary was a mere $13,500 in St. Louis. The Cardinals gave Musial a $5,000 raise in August, but he wouldn't have left St. Louis regardless of what happened.

"Back in my day, we didn't think about money as such," Musial said years later. "We enjoyed playing the game. We loved baseball. Money was kind of secondary, really."

> MUSIAL CEMENTED HIS REPUTATION AS THE MAN IN THE SECOND HALF OF THE '46 SEASON TO LEAD ST. LOUIS PAST BROOKLYN FOR THE NATIONAL LEAGUE PENNANT.

FIRST TIME FOR EVERYTHING

THE ST. LOUIS Browns entered the 1944 season with a long, depressing history as an American League doormat. They had finished higher than sixth place only once in the previous 12 seasons, and were only five years removed from a 111-loss debacle.

But the novel circumstances governing the '44 season gave the Browns reason to hope. While more than 300 Big Leaguers were off serving in World War II, the St. Louis roster had been relatively untouched. Pitcher Steve Sundra was the only Brown who had left the team for military duty. Given the diluted talent on rosters across the league, optimism for Browns fans seemed most reasonable.

Manager Luke Sewell assessed the AL rosters during Spring Training, and told his players they had a legitimate chance to win the pennant. "He said it so many times we began believing him," said Browns second baseman Don Gutteridge.

Over the next six months, a patchwork team led by 23-year-old shortstop Vern Stephens and veteran starter Nels Potter staged a surprising run to 89 wins and a pennant. General Manager Bill DeWitt fortified the pitching staff by signing Alvis "Tex" Shirley and Sig Jakucki, two hard-drinking scrappers who kept things entertaining both on and off the field.

"Every night something would happen," Browns infielder Ellis Clary said. "They would get in a bar room brawl somewhere."

The Browns clinched the pennant when left fielder Chet Laabs homered twice on the final day of the regular season to beat the Yankees, then fell to the favored Cardinals in the World Series. After finishing third in 1945, the Browns lapsed back into their losing ways. They began a run of 11 straight losing seasons that survived the club's move to Baltimore in 1954.

The season that Dodgers fans nicknamed Musial, he led St. Louis to a pennant victory over Brooklyn.

CHAPTER 11
WORLD SERIES

The 1940s produced the usual array of heroes and goats in the postseason. Cardinals outfielder Enos Slaughter made a mad dash for history in the 1946 World Series, while Red Sox shortstop Johnny Pesky was blamed for hanging on to the ball too long. Brooklyn catcher Mickey Owen earned a place in infamy with a crucial passed ball in 1941, and several supporting players enjoyed their moment in the spotlight, as well. Cookie Lavagetto used his bat and teammate Al Gionfriddo relied on his glove to make their mark on the 1947 Fall Classic. When it came to October baseball in the '40s, you never knew which players would rise to the occasion.

TRUCKIN'

DETROIT TIGERS PITCHER Virgil Trucks logged only five regular-season innings in 1945 before taking a star turn against the Chicago Cubs in the World Series, but he didn't lack for competition that summer. While finishing up his stint in the U.S. Navy, he played in service games with and against such luminaries as Joe and Dom DiMaggio, Phil Rizzuto and Johnny Mize.

"They would just take a bulldozer and scrape off a diamond and put down the lines," Trucks said in a 2000 interview. "Johnny Mize hit so many home runs into that Pacific Ocean, there are probably still some lying around there."

When his tour ended in late September, Trucks rejoined the Tigers and made history, becoming the answer to a trivia question as the first pitcher to start a World Series game after a winless regular season.

After receiving word that he had been discharged, Trucks caught a train from a Navy camp in Oklahoma to St. Louis, where the Tigers were playing the Browns with a spot in the World Series at stake. Trucks pitched 5.1 effective innings in a no-decision, and Hank Greenberg hit a grand slam to give Detroit a 6-3 victory for the American League pennant.

Four days later, Trucks pitched a complete game to beat the Cubs, 4-1, in Game 2 of the World Series. He was ineffective in his next appearance, but Detroit went on to win the Series in seven games. Trucks received a check for $3,300, or half a winner's share, for his contribution to the title.

While in the service, Trucks kept his game sharp by playing in military exhibition games before pitching for the Tigers in the 1945 World Series.

WORLD SERIES

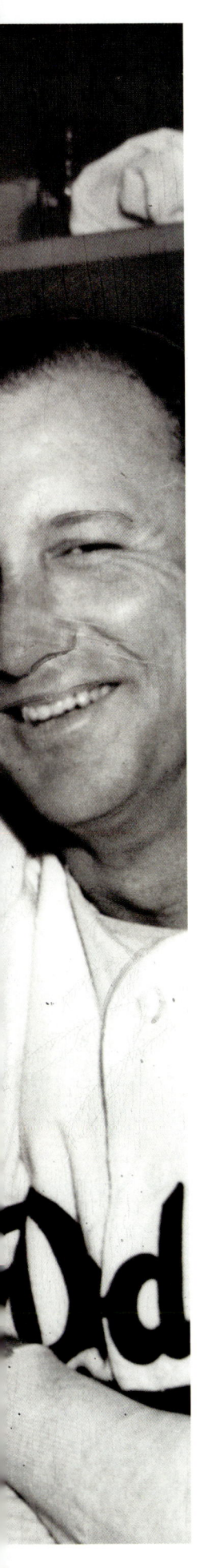

COOKIE CRUMBLES A NO-NO

Harry Arthur "Cookie" Lavagetto collected 945 regular-season hits in the Major Leagues and two more in the World Series. With the last of those knocks, a double in October 1947, Lavagetto crushed Bill Bevens' spirit and guaranteed himself one final lasting memory as a ballplayer.

Lavagetto and Bevens, two players accustomed to performing outside the glare of stardom, squeezed a lifetime's worth of drama into their confrontation in Game 4 of the World Series between the Dodgers and Yankees. *Life* magazine called it the "Most Exciting Two Minutes In World Series History."

Bevens, New York's starting pitcher, held the Dodgers hitless for eight innings despite persistent wildness. Clinging to a 2-1 lead in the ninth, Bevens retired Bruce Edwards and Spider Jorgensen on flyball outs, but he also issued two walks — his ninth and 10th of the day. With the game on the line, Brooklyn Manager Burt Shotton called on Lavagetto, a veteran contact hitter who had appeared in just 41 games all season, to pinch-hit for second baseman Eddie Stanky.

Lavagetto swung and missed at the first pitch, then drove a double off the right-field wall. Pinch-runners Al Gionfriddo and Eddie Miksis scored to give Brooklyn a 3-2 victory and send Ebbets Field into a frenzy.

The Yankees came back to win the Series in seven games, and the two principals in the drama called it a career. Bevens made a relief appearance in Game 7 and never pitched again in the Big Leagues. Lavagetto retired as a player after the '47 season and later returned as a coach in Brooklyn and as manager of the Washington Senators.

In one of Lavagetto's final career plate appearances, he struck out against New York's Spec Shea to end Game 5, a 2-1 Brooklyn loss. "Next day he was a Bum again," wrote *Life*.

> LAVAGETTO AND BEVENS, TWO PLAYERS ACCUSTOMED TO PEFORMING OUTSIDE THE GLARE OF STARDOM, SQUEEZED A LIFETIME'S WORTH OF DRAMA INTO THEIR CONFRONTATION IN GAME 4 OF THE SERIES. *LIFE* MAGAZINE CALLED IT THE "MOST EXCITING TWO MINUTES IN WORLD SERIES HISTORY."

FREE PASS

Shortly after the 1941 World Series, Brooklyn Dodgers catcher Mickey Owen returned home to his Missouri farm and sold a herd of goats and replaced them with cattle. Owen denied that the transaction was meant to help him forget the most dispiriting moment of his career, but as symbolic gestures go, it was a classic.

Long before Ralph Branca, Bill Buckner and Donnie Moore earned lasting ignominy as October goats, Owen bore the burden of failure on the national stage when it mattered most.

With the Dodgers up, 4-3, and on the verge of tying the Series at two games apiece, Hugh Casey struck out the Yankees' Tommy Henrich for the apparent final out. But the ball eluded Owen and rolled to the backstop. Henrich reached first safely and the Yankees had new life.

Lavagetto (center) ended Bill Bevens' bid for a no-hitter with a ninth-inning double that won Game 4 of the 1947 World Series.

"When you give the Yankees a reprieve, they get up out of the chair and electrocute the warden," wrote columnist Henry McLemore. A rattled Casey allowed a single to Joe DiMaggio, a Charlie Keller double, a walk and a Joe Gordon double, and before the Dodgers knew what hit them, they had lost the game, 7-4. The next day, the Yankees beat the Dodgers, 3-1, to close out the Series.

Owen, a .255 hitter who was known more for his defense than his bat, went on to play eight more seasons in the Big Leagues with the Dodgers, Cubs and Red Sox. He later worked as a coach and a scout before returning to Missouri and winning election to the office of Greene County sheriff.

Owen reflected on his famous misplay with patience and good humor whenever reporters called him and asked him to relive it.

"I don't mind," he said in 1988. "It made me famous."

ON THE AIR

Before the World Series became a nationally televised spectacle that dominated the sports landscape each October, Major League Baseball had to endure some growing pains with the new technology.

The first televised Series in 1947 featured the Yankees and Dodgers and aired in several East Coast markets, including New York, Philadelphia, Washington, D.C., and Schenectady, N.Y. Of the estimated 3.9 million viewers, the vast majority watched the games in bars.

The broadcast crew consisted of Bob Edge, Bob Stanton and Bill Slater, who called the games from a hanging cage near the mezzanine section because they weren't allowed in the press box. Radio was the preferred medium for most fans, but the dynamic changed markedly in 1950, when Commissioner Happy Chandler sold the TV rights for the All-Star Game and World Series to Gillette and the Mutual Broadcasting System for $6 million. The marriage between baseball and television was officially pronounced.

THE MAD DASH

Cardinals outfielder Enos Slaughter was touch-and-go for the final two games of the 1946 World Series because of a potentially serious injury. He had been hit in the elbow with a fastball by Boston's Joe Dobson in Game 5, and the Cardinals' medical staff advised him not to play because he risked hemorrhaging and possible amputation if he were struck on the elbow again.

Slaughter played the next two games virtually one handed. But to the Cardinals' relief, there was nothing wrong with his legs.

Slaughter collected 2,383 hits in the Major Leagues, made 10 All-Star teams and reached the Hall of Fame through the Veterans Committee in 1985. But his most memorable moment in baseball came with a 270-foot "mad dash" around the bases in the deciding Game 7 of that '46 Series.

With the Cardinals and Red Sox tied, 3-3, in the bottom of the eighth inning, Slaughter led off with a single against reliever Bob Klinger. Two outs later, he was running on the pitch when teammate Harry Walker blooped a hit to left-center field.

Leon Culberson, who had replaced the injured Dom DiMaggio in center field, came up throwing, but not quickly enough to get the hustling Slaughter. Boston shortstop Johnny Pesky hesitated briefly with the relay throw and Slaughter crossed home plate to give the Cardinals a 4-3 lead. When Harry Brecheen retired the Red Sox in the ninth, St. Louis celebrated its championship.

Brooklyn pitcher Hugh Casey (second from right) celebrates with fans following a win in the 1947 Series — the first televised Fall Classic ever. The Yankees eventually won in seven games.

THE WORLD SERIES

Slaughter slides into home to score the go-ahead — and ultimately World Series–winning — run for St. Louis in 1946.

Slaughter later said that he was determined to be aggressive after third base coach Mike Gonzalez held him up too quickly and prevented him from scoring earlier in the Series.

"A lot of people have asked me on that play, 'Was it the biggest thrill of your baseball career?'" Slaughter said. "To me, it was just a routine play as far as baseball is concerned."

ENOS SLAUGHTER'S 1946 WORLD SERIES STATS

AVG	BB	HBP	HR	2B	3B	R	RBI	OBP	SLG
.320	4	1	1	1	1	5	2	.433	.560

STREETCAR DESIRE

With travel restrictions in place because of World War II, St. Louis's two baseball teams canceled their usual Spring Training trips to Florida and held their 1944 workouts much closer to home. The Cardinals traveled to Cairo, Ill., and the Browns worked out in southeast Missouri in the town of Cape Girardeau.

George McQuinn scores after hitting a two-run homer that gave the Browns a win in Game 1 of the 1944 Series for St. Louis.

Seven months later, the teams converged back home with considerably more at stake.

Since the inaugural World Series in 1903, New York and Chicago had been the only cities to place two teams in the Fall Classic at once. St. Louis made it three in '44, when the Cardinals and Browns played in what became known as the "Streetcar Series."

The Cardinals, National League champions the previous two years, lost outfielders Enos Slaughter and Terry Moore to military service, but still boasted a talented roster with the likes of Stan Musial, Marty Marion, Max Lanier and brothers Mort and Walker Cooper.

The Browns, perennial American League doormats, stunned the baseball world behind an array of journeymen in their 30s and younger players who had been classified as ineligible for military service.

The entire World Series was played at Sportsman's Park in St. Louis. The upstart Browns captured two of the first three games behind starting pitchers Denny Galehouse and Jack Kramer, but Musial homered to lead the Cardinals to a 5-1 victory in Game 4, and the Cards put away the Browns in six games.

1944 WORLD SERIES
- GAME 1: Browns 2, Cardinals 1
- GAME 2: Browns 2, Cardinals 3 (11 innings)
- GAME 3: Cardinals 2, Browns 6
- GAME 4: Cardinals 5, Browns 1
- GAME 5: Cardinals 2, Browns 0
- GAME 6: Browns 1, Cardinals 3

"That's the fifth world championship we have won, but it's the greatest because it was local," said Cardinals President Sam Breadon. "Boy, if we had lost that one, we'd have had to leave town."

A DEER IN THE SPOTLIGHT

JOE DIMAGGIO'S PERSONAL code of conduct forbade public displays of emotion on the ball field. During the 1947 World Series, an obscure Brooklyn Dodgers outfielder robbed him of extra bases with a catch so improbable, even the stoic Yankee Clipper couldn't conceal his disappointment.

With the Yankees trailing, 8-5, in the sixth inning of Game 6, DiMaggio hit a long drive to left-center field that looked like a game-tying, three-run homer. But Dodgers outfielder Al Gionfriddo, inserted by Manager Burt Shotton as a defensive replacement, raced to the Yankee Stadium visitors' bullpen and made a remarkable catch at the 415-foot mark. DiMaggio, clearly stunned, kicked the dirt in disgust as he approached second base.

Joltin' Joe had been done in by the unlikeliest of heroes. Gionfriddo, a native of Dysart, Pa., was known as the "Dysart Deer" for his speed. But he stood only 5 foot 6, 165 pounds, and he was a career backup with the exception of a 122-game stint with the Pittsburgh Pirates in 1945.

The catch wasn't merely the highlight of Gionfriddo's career; it marked his final game in the Major Leagues. He returned to Montreal in the International League in 1948 and spent nine years in the Minor Leagues before retiring at the age of 34.

Hollywood paid tribute to the moment in the 1989 movie *Dad*, when a dying Jack Lemmon recalled Gionfriddo's catch in a conversation with his son, played by Ted Danson. Lemmon's character said the play proved that, "In America, anything is possible if you show up for work."

THE HUMAN ELEMENT

BOB FELLER'S HALL-OF-FAME resume includes one notable soft spot: He made two career starts in the World Series and went 0-2 with a 5.02 ERA against the Boston Braves in 1948. His best opportunity to win a postseason game was undermined by an umpire's errant call in the Series opener.

With the game in a scoreless tie in the eighth inning, Feller picked off pinch-runner Phil Masi at second base, but umpire Bill Stewart incorrectly ruled Masi safe. Moments later, Tommy Holmes delivered a two-out RBI single, and that proved to be the decisive run as Feller lost to Braves ace Johnny Sain, 1-0.

Feller pitched poorly in his next start, an 11-5 loss in Game 5, but he took solace in the fact that the Indians won the Series in six games. "I pitched one good game and one bad game," Feller said in a 1998 interview. "As my dad said, 'You can't saw sawdust.' That's history. You can't change it."

146

CHAPTER 12
EMOTIONAL MOMENTS

Baseball's most enduring memories aren't always forged between the lines. During a seven-year span in the 1940s, devoted fans said goodbye to New York Yankees icons Lou Gehrig and Babe Ruth. Weakened by illness and brimming with emotion in their final years, these players had mustered an inner strength that brought legions of admirers to tears. Beyond the headlines, Negro Leagues great Josh Gibson and Cincinnati Reds catcher Willard Hershberger struggled with inner demons that were impossible to overcome. The troubled ballplayers died too soon, leaving behind a trail of unanswered questions and painful what-ifs.

FALL OF THE IRON HORSE

AFTER LOU GEHRIG'S death on June 2, 1941, New York City Mayor Fiorello La Guardia decreed that flags in the city would be flown at half-staff. President Franklin Roosevelt sent flowers to Gehrig's widow, Eleanor, and many baseball stars and dignitaries weighed in with Gehrig-related reminiscences in the next day's edition of *The New York Times*.

Yankees teammate Babe Ruth remembered him as a "clean ballplayer" who "would never quit and was always in there fighting for the team to win." Young center fielder Joe DiMaggio struggled with the loss of a friend and mentor.

"He was a wonderful ballplayer and a great individual," DiMaggio said of Gehrig. "He was a good influence to us young ballplayers, to whom he was an inspiration."

Gehrig had been a rock in the middle of the Yankees' batting order since taking over for Wally Pipp as the team's regular first baseman on June 2, 1925. Over the next 14 seasons, Gehrig remained in the lineup through injuries, slumps and every other obstacle that might come his way, until he had appeared in an astonishing 2,130 consecutive games, establishing a record that would last for 56 years and earning him the nickname the "Iron Horse."

Gehrig's unprecedented streak finally ended on May 2, 1939, after his performance had regressed to the point that he approached skipper Joe McCarthy and offered to bench himself. During a subsequent visit to the Mayo Clinic, Gehrig was diagnosed with amyotrophic lateral sclerosis, a disease of the nerve cells in the brain and spinal cord. ALS took a quick and brutal toll, and Gehrig died two years later at age 37.

Following his death, Yankees great Gehrig was memorialized with a monument in the Yankee Stadium outfield.

EMOTIONAL MOMENTS

A month after Gehrig's passing, the Yankees honored him with a monument in Monument Park beyond the center-field fence at Yankee Stadium, and a year later, actor Gary Cooper starred as Gehrig in *The Pride of the Yankees*, Hollywood's ode to Gehrig's exemplary life and valiant struggle against ALS. The film was nominated for 11 Academy Awards.

THE LUCKIEST MAN

In between games of a doubleheader on July 4, 1939 — two years before his death in 1941 and just a few months after announcing his retirement due to a mysterious illness that was quickly taking his life — Lou Gehrig addressed the crowd at Yankee Stadium. On hand to celebrate what the Yankees called "Lou Gehrig Appreciation Day" were his teammates from the 1927 "Murderers' Row" club and New York City Mayor Fiorello La Guardia. During a ceremony to retire the Iron Horse's No. 4 jersey, the first to enter Monument Park, things got emotional — Yankees Manager Joe McCarthy, with whom Gehrig was close, tearfully introduced him to the 61,808 fans in attendance — before Gehrig bravely stepped to the microphone.

He spoke briefly but slowly, humbly counting the blessings in his life in the face of his overwhelming misfortune and thanking the fans who supported him throughout his career. "Fans, for the past two weeks you've been reading about a bad break," he said. "Yet today I consider myself the luckiest man on the face of the earth."

THE TURMOIL WITHIN

WILLARD HERSHBERGER HAD a short and relatively nondescript career as a Big League catcher with the Cincinnati Reds. He was known as a solid contact hitter, but with 63 games in a single season accounting for his career high, he was never more than a backup. Off the field, Hershberger earned a notable and tragic distinction: With the possible exception of Ed Delehanty, Hershberger remains the only Major Leaguer to take his own life during a season.

The Reds received the stunning news from Manager Bill McKechnie after a doubleheader against the Boston Braves on Aug. 3, 1940. When Hershberger failed to report to the ballpark, traveling secretary Gabe Paul called his room to check on his whereabouts. Hershberger said he was ill, but agreed to come to the game and watch from the stands in street clothes. After hanging up the phone, Hershberger went into the bathroom and took his own life. He was just 30 years old.

Details eventually began to emerge about Hershberger's troubled life. When he was 18 years old, his father killed himself with a shotgun, and young Willard found the body. Hershberger's Cincinnati teammates regarded him as moody and prone to exhaustive self-analysis. Just days before the suicide, Hershberger had replaced the injured Ernie Lombardi at catcher. He put excessive pressure on himself to perform in his new role and had difficulty dealing with setbacks.

Although the Reds banded together to win the NL pennant in 1940, the sting of Hershberger's death would linger.

"Hersh was a different person, kind of a recluse," teammate Eddie Joost said. "You never knew what he was thinking, and I don't think we'll ever know what really happened to him."

LEFT BEHIND

JOSH GIBSON'S DEATH in 1947 is shrouded in mystery. The only certainty is that Gibson, known to some as the "black Babe Ruth," passed from the scene long before his time. Some baseball historians believe that he was a victim of drug and alcohol abuse, while Gibson's friends maintain that he died as the result of a brain tumor.

Gibson, a power-hitting catcher with massive arms and a barrel chest, ranked among the Negro Leagues' most feared sluggers for many years. But he was also a burdened soul, and

Hershberger took his own life at age 30, unable to deal with the demons of his past.

Considered one of the best hitters ever, Gibson died three months before Jackie Robinson broke the Majors' color barrier.

EMOTIONAL MOMENTS

the accounts of his later years made reference to substance abuse and bouts of depression. He spent much of the 1943 season in a Washington, D.C., hospital, and Homestead Grays Manager Cumberland Posey said he suffered a nervous breakdown.

Gibson was reportedly heartbroken when Brooklyn Dodgers General Manager Branch Rickey targeted Jackie Robinson as the player to break the Major Leagues' color barrier. Gibson had been the Negro Leagues' standard bearer for more than a decade with the Grays and the Pittsburgh Crawfords, but Rickey thought Robinson was more temperamentally suited to the taunts and unrelenting scrutiny he would undoubtedly receive as the game's first African-American player.

Gibson, plagued by liver and kidney disease and numerous other medical demons, was 35 years old when he died on Jan. 20, 1947. Three months later, Robinson made his Big League debut with Brooklyn.

In 1972, Gibson posthumously reached his ultimate destination with election to the Baseball Hall of Fame. He followed Satchel Paige as the second player who primarily played in the Negro Leagues to make it to Cooperstown.

A HERO'S FAREWELL

GEORGE HERMAN "BABE" Ruth was just 52 years old when he showed up at Yankee Stadium on April 27, 1947, to be honored by his friends, former teammates and 58,339 fans who gathered at Yankee Stadium in the Bronx to celebrate the life of a legend. He bore scant resemblance to the boisterous, congenial "Bambino" who had launched a record 714 career home runs, thrilled crowds and terrorized opposing pitchers throughout the game as baseball's premier slugger.

It was Babe Ruth Day across baseball, and the game's home run king, in the later stages of a lengthy fight against cancer, was so weak that he could barely make it up the dugout steps to address the sellout crowd.

"Ruth moved with the uncertain slowness of the sick," wrote *New York Post* columnist Jimmy Cannon. "The camel's hair coat blew loosely in the draught and there was no belly beneath his belt. The collar of the green shirt billowed out from the emaciated neck and the cigar was out in his left hand. The tan on his face seemed unnatural because he didn't look like a man who had been out in the sun."

Ruth, his voice raspy and strained, gave a brief speech extolling the virtues of baseball, which he described as "The only real game — I think — in the world." He returned to Yankee Stadium a year later to have his No. 3 jersey retired, and died on Aug. 16, 1948, at the age of 53.

For two days, Ruth's body lay in state at the main entrance to Yankee Stadium, and an estimated 100,000 fans and admirers waited in line to celebrate his greatness and pay their final respects.

TRAGEDY

THE NATION WAS beginning to heal after the long, intense grind of World War II, and baseball was also returning to a state of normalcy in 1946, as players returned en masse from war service. But a traumatic event in June served as a stark reminder of the fragility of life even in a time of peace.

On June 24, a Washington Motor Coach bus carrying 15 members of the Class-B Spokane Indians was traveling through the Cascade Mountain Range to Bremerton, Wash., when tragedy struck. Bus driver Gus Berg swerved to avoid an oncoming car, and the bus

Ruth's admirers got one last chance to pay their respects when he was laid in state outside Yankee Stadium for two days following his death in 1948.

plunged from the Snoqualmie Pass highway into the valley below and burst into flames, killing nine team members.

Player-manager Mel Cole, shortstop George Risk, second baseman Fred Martinez, pitchers Bob Kinnaman and George Lyden, outfielders Bob James and Bob Paterson, infielder Vic Picetti and catcher Chris Hartje all perished in the deadliest accident ever involving a U.S. professional baseball team.

One crash survivor earned a morbid distinction: Infielder Jack Lohrke received word during a lunch stop on the road that he had been promoted to Triple-A San Diego, so he gathered his gear, left his teammates and hitched a ride back to Spokane. Lohrke, who had also survived the D-Day invasion and the Battle of the Bulge during World War II, eventually made the Major Leagues with the New York Giants, belting 11 home runs as a 23-year-old rookie in 1947. Lohrke would play seven total seasons, ending his Big League career with the Phillies. Until his death in 2009 at age 85, he went by the nickname "Lucky."

The accident generated a deep and profound sense of sadness throughout the country. Major League Baseball donated $25,000 from the All-Star Game to crash survivors and the families of the deceased, and entertainers Bob Hope and Bing Crosby were among those who made contributions.

> **INFIELDER JACK LOHRKE RECEIVED WORD DURING A LUNCH STOP ON THE ROAD THAT HE HAD BEEN PROMOTED. UNTIL HIS DEATH, HE WENT BY THE NICKNAME "LUCKY."**

RUST-PROOF

AFTER FOUR YEARS of military service, during which he lost several of his prime baseball years, slugger Hank Greenberg rejoined the Detroit Tigers in early July 1945 and quickly proved that rust would not be an issue. In his first game back, the All-Star slugger hit an eighth-inning home run to lead Detroit to a 9-5 victory over the Philadelphia Athletics. Later that season — after which he would finish 14th in MVP voting despite playing in just 78 games — Greenberg would display an even bigger flair for the dramatic.

On the final day of the regular season, Detroit sported an 87-65 record and a one-game lead over Washington in the American League pennant race. The Tigers needed to win one game in a doubleheader against the Browns to clinch a trip to the World Series against the Chicago Cubs.

On a dreary, rainy day in St. Louis, a meager crowd of 5,582 showed up at Sportsman's Park. After George McQuinn's RBI double gave the Browns a 3-2 lead in the bottom of the eighth inning, the wet conditions and looming darkness left the nightcap in doubt for the desperate Tigers.

That's when Greenberg came to the rescue for Detroit. With the bases loaded and one out, he drove a Nels Potter pitch over the left-field fence for a grand slam, giving the Tigers a 6-3 lead in the top of the ninth inning. Right-hander Al Benton, who also was in his first year back after missing the 1943–44 seasons while serving in the Navy, retired the Browns to end the game, and the Tigers celebrated a pennant. Afterward, Greenberg told reporters that his mind had flashed back to his war service during his climactic home run trot.

"It was the strangest thing," he said. "I wasn't sure if I was awake or dreaming."

After missing three-plus seasons, Greenberg's skills proved sharp when he helped propel the Tigers to the pennant.

SOURCE NOTES

INTRODUCTION

7. "Feller threw a fastball 104 mph to beat a motorcycle." Mitsch, Pat. "Velocity still big part of a pitcher's arsenal'" *Pittsburgh Tribune Review*. 28 June 2009.

7. "Aaron drew inspiration from Robinson's Brooklyn debut.'" Crasnick, Jerry. "Guts & Glory." *Denver Post*. 14 April 1997. Sports: P. D1.

CHAPTER 1

9. "Jimmy Breslin called DiMaggio the personification of baseball." Pluto, Terry. "American Icon Dies: 'Greatest Ballplayer' Left Mark. Generations Remember Man who Ran with 'Unhurried Grace.'" *Akron (Ohio) Beacon Journal*. 9 March 1999. Sports: A1.

10. "Williams told reporters, 'I'll play.'" Markusen, Bruce. *Ted Williams: A Biography*. Greenwood Publishing Group. 2004. P. 35.

10. "Greenberg urged the Pirates to give Kiner more time." Carchidi, Sam. "Earlier Slugging Duels are Recalled/There Were Ralph Kiner and Johnny Mize in 1947." *Philadelphia Inquirer*. 9 September 1998. P. D2A.

10. "Greenberg took Kiner under his wing and became his mentor." Kurlansky, Mark. "Hank Greenberg: The Hero Who Didn't Want to Be One." *Yale University Press*. 2011. P. 117.

13. "Kiner called Greenberg's death the saddest news he could have heard." *Pittsburgh Post-Gazette*. "Hank Greenberg's Good Deeds*; How First Baseman Hank Greenberg, an Accidental Pirate, was a Light unto Baseball." 27 September 2009. P. B7.

13. "Mel Ott's first career home run was a gift." Heuschkel, David. "The Original Giants' Masterpiece; Swing Didn't Match Slugger's Size." *Hartford Courant*. 13 August 2007. P. C6.

13. "Ott had a premonition before home run No. 500." Buck, Al. "He's Ott to trot! Giant legend first in NL to 500-home run mark." The *New York Post*. 31 July 2005. P. 54.

13. "Foxx had 'muscles in his muscles.'" Allen, Bob, with Gilbert, Bill. "The 500 Home Run Club: Baseball's 15 Greatest Home Run Hitters from Aaron to Williams." Sports Publishing, Inc. 1999. P. 39.

13. "Mel Harder called Foxx the most powerful hitter he ever saw." Allen, Bob, with Gilbert, Bill. "The 500 Home Run Club: Baseball's 15 Greatest Home Run Hitters from Aaron to Williams." Sports Publishing, Inc. 1999. P. 52.

13. "Foxx was plagued by problems off the field." Heuschkel, David. "XX Marked the Spot; Few Ballparks Could Contain Foxx's Prodigious Drives." *Hartford Courant*. 10 August 2007. P. C1.

17. "Paul Waner wanted to celebrate his 3,000th hit with a party." Anderson, Chris. "Three set to reach historic milestone." *Sarasota Herald-Tribune*. 4 April 199. P. 1K.

17. "Casey Stengel joked about Waner's grace in sliding." Parker, Clifton Blue. "Big and Little Poison: Paul and Lloyd Waner, Baseball Brothers." McFarland & Co., Inc. 2003. P. 232.

18. "Tommy Holmes was beloved by Braves fans." Heller, Dick. "Making case for Holmes' legacy." *Washington Times*. 22 April 2008. P. C4.

18. "Stephens never received the attention he deserved." Krikorian, Doug. "Stephens stood out." *Long Beach (Cal.) Press-Telegram*. 14 September 2005.

18. "Pete Reiser was carried off the field on a stretcher 11 times." Sherrod, Blackie. "Old-timer took licking, kept ticking." *Dallas Morning News*. 26 March 1993. P. 1b.

18. "Reiser had an unconquerable spirit." Smith, Red. "Harold Patrick Reiser." *The New York Times*. 2 November 1981. Section C; P. 10.

18. "Leo Durocher compared Pete Reiser to Mays." Sherrod, Blackie. "Old-timer took licking, kept ticking." *Dallas Morning News*. 26 March 1993. P. 1b.

21. "Willie Mays owed a debt of gratitude to Artie Wilson." House, Kelly. "Artie Wilson, star of the Negro Leagues and Portland Beavers, dies at 90. Forever a baseball man. Named to PCL Hall of Fame in 2003." *The Oregonian*. 1 November 2010.

21. "Buck Leonard called O'Neil one of the finest players he had seen." Negro League Baseball Players Association official Web site. NLBPA.com.

21. "Crutchfield respected O'Neil in the clutch." Negro League Baseball Players Association official Web site. NLBPA.com.

21. "Ted Williams called Doerr 'The Silent Captain of the Red Sox.'" Buckley, Steve. "The Silent Captain' still; Doerr's quiet grace and humility belie the Sox legend's greatness." 22 May 2005. P. B16.

21. "Doerr and Gordon shared roots in Oregon." Meehan, Brian. "At 89, Hall of Famer Bobby Doerr still lives on the Rogue with his memories and love of life. An Oregon treasure still sparkles. 'As close to heaven as you can get.'" *The Sunday Oregonian*. 7 October 2007. P. C1.

CHAPTER 2

25. "The weather was grim the day of Feller's no-hitter." Manoloff, Dennis. "Feller: An Opening Day gem. He started 1940 with a no-hitter; he's still going strong in 2010." *Cleveland Plain Dealer*. 5 April 2010. P. A1.

27. "Feller didn't have his best stuff against the White Sox." Manoloff, Dennis. "Feller: An Opening Day gem. He started 1940 with a no-hitter; he's still going strong in 2010." *Cleveland Plain Dealer*. 5 April 2010. P. A1.

27. "Paige said play had to be halted to clear straw hats from the field." Tye, Larry. *Satchel: The Life and Times of an American Legend*. Random House. 2009. P. 249.

27. "Details of the Paige-Gibson encounter were embellished." Tye, Larry. *Satchel: The Life and Times of an American Legend*. Random House. 2009. P. 250.

27. "Van Robays said, "Eephus ain't nothin.'" Stone, Larry. "Teddy Ballgame: King of Swing All-star memories." *Seattle Times*. 15 May 2001. P. D1.

28. "Ted Williams homered off the 'oophus' in the All-Star Game." Edes, Gordon. "Ted ripped into this one; Sewell was thrown for a loop when Williams connected on his eephus pitch in 1946." *Boston Globe*. 2 April 1999. P. C11.

30. "Hal Newhouser became a Tigers fan during the 1935 World Series." Vincent, Charlie. "Newhouser's No. 16 will hang around forever in Tigers history." *Detroit Free Press*. 25 July 1997.

30. "George Kell rated Newhouser as a great pitcher despite the competition."

30 "Lefty Grove had a short temper and a quick trigger." Mink, Michael. "Lefty Grove Earned His Way Atop Baseball's Mound Fire Strikes: The pitcher's focus and drive led to 300 victories — and the Philadelphia Athletics to two World Series titles." *Investor's Business Daily*. 6 June 2007. P. A4.

30. "Grove said they would have to 'cut the uniform" off him before he would quit." Amore, Dom. "300th Wynn; It Took Him 8 Tries; How 5 Legends Joined the Club."

30. "Grove retired on Pearl Harbor Day." Down, Fred. "Games Within The Game; Grove's Percentage Best Among 300-game Winners." United Press International. Sports News. 8 August 1985.

33. "Red Barrett was self-confident and carefree." *The Sporting News*. 13 August 1990.

33. "Barrett described himself as 'no striker-outer.'" Davis, Sid. Society for American Baseball Research, Baseball Biography Project. Bioproj.SABR.org.

33. "Johnny Murphy went by the nickname 'Grandma.'" Vorperian, John. Society for American Baseball Research, Baseball Biography Project. Bioproj.SABR.org.

33. "Hilton Smith was Satchel Paige's relief." Phillips, Mike. "Smith Finally Gets His Due." *Miami Herald*. 12 August 2001. P. 14C.

33. "Sportswriter W.C. Heinz recalled the drama when Joe Page entered a game." Vaccaro, Mike. "Ahead of His Time — Page a Pioneer in the 'Pen." The *New York Post*. 30 March 2006. P. 64.

CHAPTER 3

35. "Toots Shor played a role in DiMaggio's $100,000 contract." Anderson, Dave. "Sports of the Times; Mattingly: Yankees' Last Tradition." *The New York Times*. 11 April 1990. P. A21.

35. "DiMaggio was troubled by numerous ailments." Cramer, Richard Ben. *Joe DiMaggio: The Hero's Life*. Simon & Schuster. 2000. P. 255.

36. "The Cubs became first team to wear sleeveless uniforms." Edes, Gordon. "The 'sleeveless look' is back. Marlins expanding on baseball's fashion statement." *Ft. Lauderdale Sun-Sentinel*. 9 July 1992. P. 9C.

36. "Caribbean Series was brainchild of Oscar Prieto and Pablo Morales." Goldstein, Kevin. "2006 Caribbean Series preview." *Baseball America*. 2 February 2006.

36. "Mota, Carty, Alomar and Ortiz among the big names." Hispanic PR Wire. HispanicPRWire.com.

36. "Boudreau wanted to station an outfielder in the right-field seats." Leyden, John G. "50 years ago, baseball took a right turn; Tribe player-manager created historic 'Boudreau shift' to stop Ted Williams." *Cleveland Plain Dealer*. 20 July 1996. P. 6D.

36. "Boudreau thought Williams was 'having a carnival.'" Gano, Rick. "Lou Boudreau: Pioneering Player-Manager of the Cleveland Indians." The Associated Press. 29 July 1994. Sports News.

40. "Williams refused to tamper with his style." Heller, Dick. "Defense shifted for Ted." *Washington Times*. 17 July 2006. P. C5.

40. "Bush was a line-drive hitter." Crasnick, Jerry. "George Bush: Yale, 1947-48. A presidential pardon in order." *Denver Post*. 5 June 1995. P. D4.

40. "Bush was standing on deck during triple play." Crasnick, Jerry. "George Bush: Yale, 1947-48. A presidential pardon in order." *Denver Post*. 5 June 1995. P. D4.

40. "Carl Stotz's inspiration came when he tripped and fell over a bush." Teatum, Ashley. "Little League has grown considerably since 1939." *The Times-Tribune* (Scranton, Pa.). 23 August 2008.

40. "Seaver, Palmer, Ryan among the famous Little Leaguers." Hillinger, Charles. "A museum piece; Stotz, 79, founded Little League, then found he could do without it when it became big business." *Los Angeles Times*. 25 August 1989. Sports; P.4.

43. "Stotz had no idea what Little League would become." Loh, Jules. "50 Years of Little League Baseball." The Associated Press. 18 August 1989. Sports News.

43. "Bud Holman brought the Dodgers to Vero Beach." Kerasotis, Peter. "Dodgertown's days long gone." *Florida Today*. 9 March 2008. P. 1D.

43. "Mota called Vero a 'place of greatness.'" Warner, Gary A. "Quick Trip: Farewell to Vero's Dodgertown; After more than 60 years at their quirky old Vero Beach ballpark, the Dodgers prepare for the final season at their Florida spring-training home." *Orange County Register*. 24 February 2008.

CHAPTER 4

45. "Roosevelt thought it was best for country to keep baseball going." Frey, Jennifer. "Through The Tears, Let's Play Ball." *Washington Post*. 17 September 2001. Style; P. C1.

45. "Death and injury toll was heavy among Major Leaguers during the war." Mullener, Elizabeth. " A Game of Their Own; A new World War II museum exhibit honors baseball's vital role in raising the morale of soldiers on the battlefield and families back home."

47. "The Reds wanted to sign Joe Nuxhall's father." Bortstein, Larry. Youth did not serve Nuxhall: In June 1944, the pitcher became the youngest player to appear in a major league game. He didn't last long." *Orange County Register*. 7 September 1994. P. D4.

47. "Nuxhall was 'scared to death' by the sight of Stan Musial." Kay, Joe. "A debut at 15: Joe Nuxhall was major leagues' youngest player." The Associated Press. 29 May 1994. Sports; P. B2.

47. "Pete Gray was proficient in the outfield, flawed as a hitter." Holtzman, Jerome. "One-armed Pete Gray's career was short and bitter." *Chicago Tribune*. 20 April 1989. Sports: P. 3C.

48. "Ellis Clary said Gray could outrun a 'scalded dog.'" Golenbock, Peter. *The Spirit of St. Louis: A History of the St. Louis Cardinals and Browns*. Avon Books. 2000. P. 313.

48. "Lou Brissie urged doctors to save his leg." Merschel, Michael. "Excerpt: 'The Corporal Was A Pitcher,' by Ira Berkow.'" Texas Pages. 29 March 2009.

48. "Grantland Rice praised Brissie as an example." Johnson, Rachel. "World War II hero adapted style to play in the Majors." *Aiken (S.C.) Standard*. 15 January 2009.

50. "Wrigley might have used the donation story as a 'smokescreen." Holtzman, Jerome, and Vass, George. *Baseball, Chicago Style. A Tale of Two Teams, One City*. Bonus Books. 2001.

53. "Hugh Mulcahy expected to be reaching his peak after the war." Heller, Dick. "Mulcahy was far from loser." *Washington Times*. 3 March 2008. P. C2.

53. "Hank Greenberg vowed to be a good soldier." Sudyk, Bob. "Prewar baseball season dulled the sound of distant guns." *Hartford Courant*. 13 October 1991. P. A1.

53. "Milton Berle appeared at three-way exhibition game." Heller, Dick. "One game, three teams in '44." *Washington Times*. 2 July 2006. P. C4.

53. "The New York Times described the game as 'lunacy.'" Sherrington, Kevin. "Season of the unseasoned; With star players off at war, Majors had decidedly minor feel in summer of '44." *Dallas Morning News*. 31 March 1994. P. 19G.

53. "Bob Feller was driving to Chicago when news of Pearl Harbor broke." Herzog, Bob. "Baseball Goes to War; As hundreds of players, including some of the greatest stars, served their country in World War II, the games went on with the blessing of FDR." *Newsday*. 9 October 2001. P. A76.

53. "Feller never regarded himself as a hero." Rozner, Barry. "He might have disagreed, but Feller a true American hero." *Chicago Daily Herald*. 19 December 2010. Sports: P. 1.

53. "*Sporting News* editorial called for a change in Spring Training." Gietschier, Steve. "It happens every spring; Even World War II couldn't stop baseball's annual preseason pageant known as

spring training." *The Sporting News.* 21 March 1994. TSN Classics; P. 6.

55. "Moe Berg was a true renaissance man." Tsuruoka, Doug. "Intelligence Agent Moe Berg; Dare To Dream: Renaissance man proved that everything is within reach." *Investor's Business Daily.* 21 November 2006. P. A3.

55. "Casey Stengel was amazed by Berg's knowledge." Tsuruoka, Doug. "Intelligence Agent Moe Berg; Dare To Dream: Renaissance man proved that everything is within reach." *Investor's Business Daily.* 21 November 2006. P. A3.

55. "Berg bailed on plan to assassinate Heisenberg." Casey, Dennis. "Jack of all trades; spies of United States." *Spokesman Magazine.* 1 March 2004.

55. "Sawamura's ship was struck by a torpedo." Gary Bedingfield's Baseball in Wartime. BaseballInWartime.com.

57. "Jackie Robinson was arrested and court-martialed for refusal to give up seat on bus." Shelburne, Ramona. "History for sale; Documents on Jackie Robinson's court-martial find their way to auction." *Daily News of Los Angeles.* 16 May 2008. P. C1.

57. "Robinson wrote a letter to Secretary of War aide." Vernon, John. "Jim Crow, Meet Lieutenant Robinson. A 1944 Court-Martial." Spring 2008, Vol. 40, No. 1.

57. "AAGPBL players were provided with lessons on etiquette and beauty." The All-American Girls Professional Baseball League official Web site. AAGPBL.org.

57. "Fans stuck around when they realized women played a good brand of ball." Fincher, Jack. "The Belles of the Game' were a hit with their fans." Smithsonian. July 1989. P. 88-97.

CHAPTER 5

61. "Casey Stengel and Stan Musial were both Mize admirers." Broeg, Bob. "Big John: As a hitter, Mize had size for power, eyes for contact." *St. Louis Post-Dispatch.* 4 June 1993. Sports; P. 4D.

61. "Campanella impressed with view of Mize from behind the plate." Eisenbath, Mike. "Big Mac mirrors Big Cat at bat, in character." *St. Louis Post-Dispatch.* 22 July 1998. Sports: D1.

61. "Musial consider Mize trade a 'terrible mistake.'" Musial, Stan, with Broeg, Bob. "The Man's memories of Mize and a bad move; When the Cardinals let The Big Cat out of the bag, they blew a dynasty." *The Sporting News.* 14 June 1993. P.7.

62. "Effa Manley developed reputation as shrewd businesswoman." Smith, Claire. "In a league of her own." *Philadelphia Inquirer.* 30 July 2006. Sports; P. D1.

62. "Manley's gravestone cited her love of baseball." Crawford, Aimee. "First Lady of Black Baseball Was the Caring Innovator in Negro Baseball Leagues." *Los Angeles Sentinel.* 27 February 2002. Vo. 67; No. 48; P. 1.

62. "Webb expressed doubts about Yankees hiring Stengel." Allen, Maury. *You Could Look It Up: The Life of Casey Stengel.* Times Books. 1979. P. 7.

62. "Stengel committed a gaffe at opening press conference." Allen, Maury. *You Could Look It Up: The Life of Casey Stengel.* Times Books. 1979. P. 7.

67. "Veeck cited three factors in big Cleveland crowds." Veeck, Bill, with Linn, Ed. *Veeck As in Wreck.* University of Chicago Press. 1962. P. 105.

67. "Indians held 'Good Old Joe Early Night' at Municipal Stadium." Veeck, Bill, with Linn, Ed. *Veeck As in Wreck.* The University of Chicago Press. 1962. P. 112.

67. "Veeck thought Arizona would be more hospitable to an African-American player." Ruelas, Richard. "Cactus League outgrowth of Fla. racial bias." *Arizona Republic.* 20 March 2010. P. E1.

69. "Breadon borrowed money to allow Haines transaction to take place." Polner, Murray. *Branch Rickey: A Biography.* McFarland & Company, Inc. 2007. P. 80.

69. "Rickey's proposal was 'revolutionary.'" Puerzer, Richard J. "Engineering baseball: Branch Rickey's innovative approach to baseball management." *Nine.* 22 September 2003. Vol. 12; P. 72 (17).

69. "Happy Chandler oversaw start of pension fund and other developments." Thomas Jr., Robert McG. "A.B. (Happy) Chandler, 92, Dies; Led Baseball During Integration." *The New York Times.* 16 June 1991. Section 1; P. 26.

69. "Chandler supported Jackie Robinson's right to play." Christl, Cliff. "Commissioners past: 8 men out of luck. From Landis to Vincent, Selig's predecessors all fell upon hard times on job." *Milwaukee Journal Sentinel.* 9 July 1998. Sports: P. 3.

CHAPTER 6

71. "The mood was initially tense during Rickey-Robinson meeting." Eig, Jonathan. *Opening Day: The Story of Jackie Robinson's First Season.* Simon & Schuster. 2007. P. 26.

71. "Rickey read a passage on non-resistance." Polner, Murray. *Branch Rickey: A Biography.* McFarland & Company, Inc. 2007. P. 152.

73. "Robinson expressed career ambition in a questionnaire." Eig, Jonathan. *Opening Day: The Story of Jackie Robinson's First Season.* Simon & Schuster. 2007. P. 28.

73. "There were empty seats in abundance for Robinson's debut." *The Hamilton Spectator* (Ontario, Canada). "Covering Jackie; Sixty years ago tomorrow, newspapers throughout North America ran the story of a black player on the Brooklyn Dodgers breaking baseball's colour barrier. Here's what they wrote." 14 April 2007.

73. "Times columnist Daley described debut as uneventful." Eig, Jonathan. *Opening Day: The Story of Jackie Robinson's First Season.* Simon & Schuster. 2007. P. 28.

73. "Clyde Sukeforth grew up as a Babe Ruth fan in Maine." Schultz, Randy. "Clyde Sukeforth: Former player, coach and scout played roles in Jackie Robinson's signing and the 1951 N.L. pennant; Turn Back The Clock." *Baseball Digest.* 1 July 2005. P. 72 (4).

73. "Sukeforth was never the same after hunting accident." Jordan, Glenn. "A humble ambassador; Clyde Sukeforth, who may have given more to baseball than any other Mainer, was best known for his quiet dignity." *Portland (Me.) Press Herald.* 6 September 2000. P. 1A.

74. "Rickey told Robinson to be aggressive in Minor League debut." *Newsday.* "Jersey City Debut." 4 March 1997. Sports; P. A65.

74. "The newspapers were filled with praise for Robinson's performance." Griffin, Richard. "Jackie Robinson: A portrait in courage. Canada was the testing site for baseball's racial experiment." *Toronto Star.* 1 June 1996. Sports; P. B5.

74. "Robinson statue was dedicated in Jersey City." Hoekstra, Dave. "A 'great city' rises in Jersey." *Chicago Sun-Times.* 4 November 2007. Travel: P. C1.

74. "Feller and Paige were an unlikely twosome." Tye, Larry. *Satchel: The Life and Times of an American Legend.* Random House. 2009. P. 171.

74. "Wrangling over money produced some hard feelings." Tye, Larry. *Satchel: The Life and Times of an American Legend.* Random House. 2009. P. 174.

74. "Feller's tour left a legacy." Gay, Timothy. *Satch, Dizzy & Rapid Robert. The Wild Sage of Interracial Baseball Before Jackie Robinson.* Simon & Schuster. 2010. P. 244.

76. "Brown took the field with 'Reader's Digest' in his pocket." Letlow, Paul. "Which Brown Would Show Up?" *The News-Star* (Monroe, La.). 27 February 2006. Sports: P. 1C.

76. "O'Neil called Brown a great natural athlete." Lewis, Ted. "He made it look easy.' Shreveport native had short stint in MLB but enshrined in Hall." *New Orleans Times-Picayune.* 16 June 2007. Sports: P. 1.

76. "Dan Bankhead was labeled the 'next Satchel Paige.'" Dolgan, Bob. "Making his pitch; Brooklyn's Dan Bankhead provided relief as baseball's first black pitcher to appear in a major-league game." *Cleveland Plain Dealer.* 30 June 1997. Sports; P. 3C.

81. "Veeck's 'plan' to buy Phillies and stock team with Negro Leaguers might have been embellished." Herrman, Mark. "Jackie Robinson 50th anniversary. A hung jury. Did Landis keep Veeck from being the first to sign black players?" *Newsday.* 13 April 1997. Sports; P. H25.

81. "Veeck and Manley reached a deal to bring Doby to Cleveland." Leonard, Tim. "The glory of his time; Doby takes back seat to no one." *Bergen Record.* 26 July 1998. Sports; P. S01.

81. "Doby never felt slighted over a lack of recognition." Davidoff, Ken. "Second to none; American League his stage; Doby was thrust into pioneer role." *Bergen Record.* 6 July 1997. Sports: P. S01.

81. "Cool Papa Bell and Josh Gibson posted big numbers in Mexico." Clark, Bill. "Mexican League gig full of 'memories and dreams." *Columbia Daily Tribune* (Missouri). 30 April 2008.

85. "Black players enjoyed a sense of equality in Mexico." Tye, Larry. *Satchel: The Life and Times of an American Legend.* Random House. 2009. P. 119.

85. "MLB attendance spiked with the arrival of black players." Keisser, Bob. "Baseball was segregated and later integrated for one overriding reason: Money." *Long Beach Press-Telegram.* 22 April 1997.

85. "Integration hastened the end of the Negro Leagues." Glauber, Bill. "Integration of Majors was death knell of Negro Leagues." *Baltimore Sun.* 13 May 1990.

CHAPTER 7

87. "Rickey tore up Musial's contract." Golenbock, Peter. *The Spirit of St. Louis: A History of the St. Louis Cardinals and Browns.* Avon Books. 2000. P. 239.

87. "Musial figured out that home run hitters drove Cadillacs."
Whiteside, Larry. "Stan the Man; For 22 years in St. Louis, Musial was the one and only." *Boston Globe.* 6 August 1994. Sports; P. 61.

87. "Brooklyn fans loved Musial." Riverfront Times interview with George Vecsey. RiverfrontTimes.com. 3 May 2011.

89. "Johnny Beazley injured his arm during an exhibition in Memphis." Golenbock, Peter. *The Spirit of St. Louis: A History of the St. Louis Cardinals and Browns.* Avon Books. 2000. P. 251.

89. "Beazley's son said he was overworked." Fry, Darrell; "Grimmer Games; In WWII, most athletes played on real battlefields." *Washington Times.* 1 December 1991. C1.

89. "Recalling the encounter between Williams and Pesky over lunch." Parrillo, Bill. "Pesky's still having fun and sharing stories at 81." *Providence Journal-Bulletin.* 25 February 2001.

92. "Williams was impressed by Pesky's feistiness." Parrillo, Bill. "Pesky's still having fun and sharing stories at 81." *Providence Journal-Bulletin.* 25 February 2001.

92. "Ashburn's early contracts were voided." Bostrom, Don. "Richie Ashburn; From Cornfield to Cooperstown." *Morning Call* (Allentown, Pa.). 28 July 1995. C1.

92. "Ted Williams referred to Ashburn as 'Putt-Putt.'" Goldstein, Richard. "Richie Ashburn, Whiz Kid and Original Met, Dies at 70." *The New York Times.* 10 September 1997. P. B8.

92. "Dick Wakefield generated comparisons to Ted Williams." Gallo, Bill. "Another phenom's short stay in bigs." New York *Daily News.* 31 August 1997. P. 83.

92. "The Tigers gave Wakefield a Cadillac." Howard-Cooper, Scott. "The Daze of Bonuses for Babies; In an Era Before the Amateur Draft, Young Prospects Were Available to the Highest Bidder." *Los Angeles Times.* 24 July 1990. P. C1.

97. "Wakefield thought the resentment came from the newspapers." Honig, Donald. *Baseball Between the Lines: Baseball in the Forties and Fifties, as Told by the Men Who Played It.* University of Nebraska Press. 1993. Pp. 80-81.

97. "Del Ennis was a target for the boos." Fitzpatrick, Frank. "Why did they boo Del Ennis?" *Philadelphia Inquirer.* 29 June 2003.

97. "Robin Roberts recalled how tough Phillies fans were on Ennis." Hagen, Paul. "Time to give slugger Del Ennis his due." *Philadelphia Daily News.* 15 April 2011. P. Main 254.

99. "Bobby Thomson was known as the Staten Island Scot." O'Leary, Daniel. "Baseball legend Bobby Thomson dies at 86." *Staten Island (N.Y.) Advance.* 18 August 2010.

99. "Gene Bearden suffered wounds during World War II." Dolgan, Bob. "Indians hero Bearden dies; Left-hander pitched team to championship in 1948." *Cleveland Plain Dealer.* 20 March 2004. P. A1.

100. "Don Newcombe had a fear of flying." *Jet Magazine.* 5 December 1957. P. 52.

100. "Newcombe helped athletes avoid the pitfalls of substance abuse." Langill, Mark. *Celebrating Black History; Don Newcombe: a Legend On and Off Field.* Sentinel. 28 February 2008. P. B2 Vol. 73.

100. "Some writers were critical when Paige signed with Cleveland." Veeck, Bill, with Linn, Ed. *Veeck As In Wreck.* The University of Chicago Press. 1962. P. 185.

100. "Paige put on a show in his debut." Tye, Larry. *Satchel: The Life and Times of an American Legend.* Random House. 2009. P. 2009.

100. "Paige made himself a Rookie of the Year candidate." Lind, Angus. "Saluting 'Satchel' Paige; One of baseball's great pitchers, he tossed off good quotes as well." *Times-Picayune.* 6 July 2005. Living: P. 1.

CHAPTER 8

103. "Feller thought it was his "right" to serve in the military." Rozner, Barry. "He might have disagreed, but Feller a true American hero." *Chicago Daily Herald.* 19 December 2010. Sports; P.1.

103. "Warren Spahn gained perspective from his war years." Hunt, Michael. "Spahn; Game's greatest lefty a complete ballplayer." *Milwaukee Journal Sentinel.* 25 November 2003. P. 1C.

103. "Spahn helped repair the bridge at Remagen." DeVault, Darl. "Super Southpaw. Hall-of-Fame Pitcher Warren Spahn Dominated Hitters." *Daily Oklahoman.* 25 October 1998. Sports: P. 4.

104. "President Eisenhower was a Mickey Vernon fan." Hawthorn, Tom. "First baseman who later coached Expos was Eisenhower's favourite ballplayer." *Globe and Mail.* 27 December 2008. P. S10.

104. "Vernon served in the Navy." Steadman, John. "In Vernon, a mean bat, gentle man." *Baltimore Sun.* 8 February 1998. P. 2C.

104. "Mickey Vernon's hometown dedicated a statue in his honor." Heller, Dick. "One final memorial for Mount Vernon." *Washington Times.* 26 September 2008. P. C1.

104. "Austrian doctor helped safe Shepard's life." Nelson, John.

The Associated Press. 29 May 1993. Sports News.

107. "A meeting with the Under Secretary of War Patterson paved the way for Shepard." Holway, John B. "Amputee Lived a Major League Dream." *Washington Post*. 30 June 1985. P. D4.

107. "Ted Williams praised Cecil Travis' ability." Schudel, Matt. "Cecil Travis; Washington Senators Legend." *Washington Post*. 22 December 2006. P. B6.

107. "Travis' skills diminished after the war." Newville, Todd. "Remembering … Cecil Travis; former All-Star shortstop hit .314 during a 12-year big league career." *Baseball Digest*. 1 May 2003. P. 58 (5); Vol. 62.

107. "Joe DiMaggio hated his time in the war." Cramer, Richard Ben. *Joe DiMaggio: The Hero's Life*. Simon & Schuster. 2000. P. 213.

109. "DiMaggio resented his military service." Jones, David. *Joe DiMaggio: A Biography*. Greenwood Press. 2004. P. 85.

109. "Williams' natural gifts made him an ideal pilot." Cataneo, David. "On this Memorial Day, Ted Williams remembers those who didn't make it home." *Boston Herald*. 26 May 1997. P. 90.

109. "Williams received deferment as sole provider for his mother." Nowlin, Bill. *Ted Williams At War*. Rounder Books. 2007. P. 18,

CHAPTER 9

111. "Encounter with DiMaggio started Patkin on road to comedy." Elderkin, Phil. "The circuit-riding clown who's made ballparks roar." *Christian Science Monitor*. 23 July 1981. Sports: P. 16.

111. "Patkin played an estimated 4,000 ballpark dates." Goldstein, Richard. "Max Patkin, 79, Clown Prince of Baseball." *The New York Times*. 1 November 1999. P. B8.

111. "Patkin enjoyed making people laugh." The Associated Press. 7 July 1989. Sports News.

112. "Giants publicist led the hype for Hartung." Kaplan, Jim. "No Ticket to Cooperstown." *Sports Illustrated*. 24 March 1980.

112. "Hartung was a classic two-way threat." King, David, "Quiet life of baseball's 'Hondo Hurricane.'" *San Antonio Express-News*. 26 February 2007. P. 1A.

112. "Walker Cooper was called 'Hog Jaws' and 'Sow Belly.'" Harris, Don, The Arizona Republic. "Walker Cooper Looks Back on An All-Star Career." *Baseball Digest*. June 1990. P. 70.

112. "Walker knew when it was time to quit." TheBaseballPage.com.

112. "Walker Cooper lamented his meager compensation." *St. Louis Post-Dispatch*. "Walker Cooper dies; All-Star catcher in '40s." 16 April 1991. P. 4C.

117. "Bill Sianis promoted his bar with the help of his goat." Stout, Glenn, and Johnson, Richard A. *The Cubs: The Complete Story of Chicago Cubs Baseball*. Houghton Mifflin Company. 2007. P. 192.

117. "Sianis sent Philip Wrigley a telegram." Thompson, Wright. "The bleat goes on; Bitter curse now rests solely on Cubs' backs." *The Kansas City Star*. 1 May 2005. P. C12.

117. "Sianis was savvy enough to play along with the Billy Goat curse." Stout, Glenn, and Johnson, Richard A. *The Cubs: The Complete Story of Chicago Cubs Baseball*. Houghton Mifflin Company. 2007. P. 193.

117. "Lou Boudreau mailed a letter to Indians Owner Alva Bradley." Berkow, Ira. "Lou Boudreau, a Longtime Player-Manager and Hall of Fame Shortstop, Dies at 84."

117. "The press poked fun at Boudreau's youth." Holtzman, Jerome. "Boudreau: Memoir of the Boy Manager." *Chicago Tribune*. 6 July 1993. P. 3. Zone: N.

119. "William Cox was a talker and a self-promoter." Holtzman, Jerome. "Turn back the clock … 1943: William Cox, the last man banned before Pete Rose." *Baseball Digest*. 1 August 2004. P. 73 (3).

119. "Bucky Harris vented to reporters after Cox fired him." Holtzman, Jerome. "Turn back the clock … 1943: William Cox, the last man banned before Pete Rose." *Baseball Digest*. 1 August 2004. P. 73 (3).

119. "Cox said his bets were 'sentimental' in nature." *Time* Magazine. "Sport: New Odds for the Phillies." 6 December 1943.

119. "Barber tried not to get his 'tenses fouled up.'" Smith, Curt. *Voice of Summer: Ranking Baseball's 101 All-Time Best Announcers*. Carroll & Graf Publishers. 2005. P. 45.

119. "Branch Rickey kept Barber in the loop about Robinson." Schaer, Sidney C. "Still In The Catbird Seat; For years, Red Barber was the smooth, knowing radio voice of the Brooklyn Dodgers, as popular as the players themselves. Now almost 80, he's still perched where he wants to be, commenting on sports." *Newsday* Magazine. 7 February 1988. P. 14.

121. "Mel Allen was the voice and conscience of Yankees." Zipay, Steve. "Mel Allen, 1913-1996. Farewell, Mel. Was Voice of Yankee Glory Days." *Newsday*. 18 June 1996. P. A67.

121. "Veeck said his antics with the fence were perfectly legal." Veeck, Bill, with Linn, Ed. *Veeck As In Wreck*. The University of Chicago Press. 1962. P. 60.

121. "Dizzy Dean said that Medwick 'don't fight fair.'" Broeg, Bob. "Medwick had to scrap both on, off field." *St. Louis Post-Dispatch*. 17 August 1997. P. 1F.

122. "Medwick and Bowman clashed in an elevator." Durocher, Leo, and Linn. Ed. *Nice Guys Finish Last*. The University of Chicago Press. 1975. P. 136.

122. "Medwick was never the same after beaning." Anderson, Dave. "Beanballs: Clemens, Piazza and Medwick." *The New York Times*. 11 July 2000. Section D, P. 2.

122. "Ted Williams blamed sportswriter Webb for MVP loss." Stout, Glenn. "The Case of the 1947 MVP ballot; Who killed Ted Williams' chance to win?" *The Sporting News*. 20 December 1993. P. 7.

122. "Other accounts cast doubts on Williams' claim." Stout, Glenn. "The Case of the 1947 MVP ballot; Who killed Ted Williams' chance to win?" *The Sporting News*. 20 December 1993. P. 7.

122. "Leo Durocher went home to California in 1947." Durocher, Leo, and Linn. Ed. *Nice Guys Finish Last*. The University of Chicago Press. 1975. P. 261.

122. "Durocher courted trouble by associating with gamblers." Broun, Heywood Hale, "'Leo the Lip' Woulda Had the Last Word.'" *The New York Times* News Service. 13 October 1991.

124. "Chandler recounted the Durocher incident in 1971." Chandler, A.B. (Happy), with Underwood, John. "Gunned Down By the Heavies: Durocher's suspension triggered Chandler's downfall. The owners didn't mind losing Leo — but they didn't want a strong commissioner." *Sports Illustrated*. 3 May 1971.

124. "Danny Gardella doubled his salary with Veracruz." Thurber, Jon. "Danny Gardella, 85; Sought Labor Rights." *Los Angeles Times*. 17 March 2005. P. B10.

124. "Gardella sued because he wanted to play." Izenberg, Jerry. "A major-league debt past due." *The Star-Ledger* (Newark, N.J.). 25 April 2005. Sports: P. 38.

124. "Arky Vaughan walked out after a dispute with Durocher." Vecsey, George. "The Arky Vaughan Stories." *The New York Times*. 31 July 1985. Section B; P. 7.

124. "Vaughan's son said he quit and went home to run the family farm." McCurdie, Jim. "Arky Vaughan; The quiet and talented shortstop was at long last welcomed into Hall of Fame — 37 years after retirement and 33 years after his death." *Los Angeles Times*. Sports: P. 21.

CHAPTER 10

129. "Birdie Tebbetts inspired the Yankees with his joke." Golenbock, Peter. *Red Sox Nation: An Unexpurgated History of the Boston Red Sox*. Triumphs Books. 2005. P. 181.

129. "A long train ride for the Boston players." Golenbock, Peter. *Red Sox Nation: An Unexpurgated History of the Boston Red Sox*. Triumphs Books. 2005. P. 182.

131. "The Cleveland papers referred to Giebell as the kid." Dolgan, Bob. "Season with surprise ending; Unknown Tiger beats Feller, Tribe to give Detroit 1940 pennant." *Cleveland Plain Dealer*. 8 May 2001. P. 1D.

131. "Del Baker had a hunch Giebell would deliver." Dolgan, Bob. "Season with surprise ending; Unknown Tiger beats Feller, Tribe to give Detroit 1940 pennant." *Cleveland Plain Dealer*. 8 May 2001. P. 1D.

131. "The Indians celebrated with a raucous team party." Pluto, Terry. "Nothing stops Tribe. Not bar fights, not hangovers, not a bad call; not even a winless Feller." *Akron Beacon Journal*. 2 August 1998. P. D1.

131. "Sox Manager McCarthy was assailed for Galehouse decision." Buckley, Steve. "McCarthy Curse may be first up for Sox." *Boston Herald*. 1 October 1995. P. B1.

132. "The '42 Dodgers blew huge lead over St. Louis." Murphy, Justin. "Baseball's Best Runners-Up: 1942 Dodgers." Seamheads.com.

132. "Musial's nickname was born in Brooklyn." Broeg, Bob. "Meet Stan the Man: Baseball's living legend — Stan Musial — makes pitchers quake and St. Louis fans cheer." *The Rotarian*. April 1963. P. 35.

134. "Musial turned down opportunity to play in Mexico." Golenbock, Peter. *The Spirit of St. Louis: A History of the St. Louis Cardinals and Browns*. Avon Books. 2000. P. 367.

134. "Manager Sewell told Browns they had a chance to win pennant." Golenbock, Peter. *The Spirit of St. Louis: A History of the St. Louis Cardinals and Browns*. Avon Books. 2000. P. 285.

134. "Browns had their share of brawls." Golenbock, Peter. *The Spirit of St. Louis: A History of the St. Louis Cardinals and Browns*. Avon Books. 2000.

CHAPTER 11

137. "Virgil Trucks played ball in the Navy." Rosenberg, Michael. "55 years after the won the World Series on the north side of Chicago, the Tigers … return to Wrigley." *Detroit Free Press*. 2 June 2000. P. 1D.

137. "Trucks received a $3,300 check." Scanlon, Dick. "Casualties of war: Baseball battle baffles former Tiger Virgil Trucks." *Lakeland (Fla.) Ledger*. 10 February 1995. P. 1D.

139. "Details of Lavagetto-Bevens matchup." Gustkey, Earl. "1947: A Series of surprising stars; Lavagetto, Bevens, and Gionfriddo had their moments." *Los Angeles Times*. 17 October 1987. Sports: Part 3; P. 1.

139. "Lavagetto-Bevens confrontation called 'Most Exciting Two Minutes in World Series History.'" *Life* Magazine. 13 October 1947.

139. "Mickey Owen went home to Missouri after World Series." D'Antonio, Michael. *Forever Blue: The True Story of Walter O'Malley, Baseball's Most Controversial Owner, and the Dodgers of Brooklyn and Los Angeles*. Riverhead Trade. 2010.

141. "Yankees made Dodgers pay for reprieve." Heller, Dick. "Owen's '41 muff doomed Dodgers." *Washington Times*. 18 July 2005. P. C3.

141. "Owen didn't mind the notoriety." Hinckley, David. "Which side are you playin' on? Mickey Owen's bad day, Oct. 5, 1941." New York *Daily News*. 10 September 2003. P. 23.

141. "Most early World Series viewers watched from bars." Owens, Jim. "Television sports milestones; A chronology of an industry." Television Broadcast. 1 July 2006. P. 42.

141. "Broadcasters weren't allowed in World Series press box." Patton, Paul. "Filling in the big picture: Pioneers helped make TV a Series business." *Globe and Mail* (Canada). 20 October 1987.

141. "Slaughter ignored medical risks to play in Series." Broeg, Bob. "Small body, big player." *St. Louis Post-Dispatch*. 13 August 2002. Sports: P. E6.

144. "Slaughter viewed mad dash as just a routine play." O'Neill, Dan. "Cardinals Hall of Famer was known for 'Mad Dash.'" *St. Louis Post-Dispatch*. 13 August 2002. P. A1.

144. "St. Louis joined New York and Chicago in exclusive club." Olson, Stan. "Subway revival." *Charlotte Observer*. 10 October 2000. 1C.

145. "Breadon ranked 1944 title as the 'greatest' for Cardinals." Eisenbath, Mike. "This week … in 1944." St. Louis Post-Dispatch." 5 October 1994. P. 2D.

145. "Gionfriddo was known as the 'Dysart Deer.'" Zant, John. "The Catch Heard 'Round the World." *Santa Barbara Independent* (California). 4 October 2007. P. 47.

145. "Hollywood paid tribute to Gionfriddo catch." Downey, Mike. "A Fall Classic; Former Dodger May Not Be Easily Remembered, but His Catch Against DiMaggio in the '47 World Series Is One of the Greatest." *Los Angeles Times*. 27 August 1997. P. C1.

145. "Feller refused to dwell on bad call." Dolgan, Bob. "His subpar season was a great year; Feller lost 15 games and got booed in 1948, but he also became a World Series champion." *Cleveland Plain Dealer*. 19 April 1998. P. 1C.

CHAPTER 12

147. "Tributes poured in after Lou Gehrig's death." La Guardia and Baseball Chiefs Pay Tribute to Gehrig's Memory; Mayor Praises Civic Contributions of Former Ball Player — Yankees Stunned by Passing of Ex-Team-mate." *The New York Times*. 3 June 1941.

148. "Reds were concerned when Hershberger failed to report to park." Heller, Dick. "Suicide marred Reds' flag in '40." *Washington Times*. 2 October 2006. P. C16.

148. "Hershberger put pressure on himself." Wigley, Brian J., Ashley, Frank B., and Le Unes, Arnold. "Willard Hershberger and the Legacy of Suicide." *The National Pastime*. 1 January 2000. Volume 20, P. 72.

148. "Joost considered Hershberger a 'recluse.'" Groeschen, Tom. "From the despair of a suicide, to the joy of a world title, it was The Reds' Wild Ride." *Cincinnati Enquirer*. 5 April 1999. P. 21S.

148. "Josh Gibson's death was shrouded in mystery." Collier, Gene. "The Slugger; Josh Gibson may be Pittsburgh's best player — ever." *Pittsburgh Post-Gazette*. 20 October 1996. P. C3.

153. "Gibson was heartbroken when Robinson broke color barrier." Clay, Gregory. "Josh Gibson's slide into sadness; Part man, part myth, 'The Black Babe Ruth' is ranked among baseball's greatest players. He also caught his share of misery." *Baltimore Sun*. 11 July 1999. P. 1C.

153. "Babe Ruth could barely climb steps to address the crowd." Cannon, Jimmy. "Cheers & tears for a legend — Babe Ruth Day Sunday, April 27, 1947. *New York Post*. 6 April 2008. P. 10.

153. "Fans waited to pay tribute to Ruth at Yankee Stadium." Montefinise, Angela. "20 greatest moments in Yankee Stadium

history." *New York Post.* 21 September 2008. P. 6.

153. "Spokane Indians' bus driver swerved to avoid a car." Stalwick, Howie. "Deadly Indians bus crash in 1946 still haunts survivor." *Idaho Statesman.* 12 August 2002. Sports; P. 1.

155. "Jack Lohrke earned the nickname 'Lucky.'" McGrath, John. " 'Lucky' Lohrke owes his life to PCL promotion." *Tacoma News Tribune.* 25 June 2006. Sports; P. C1.

155. "Bob Hope and Bing Crosby made contributions." Geranios, Nicholas K. "Baseball team celebrates centennial." The Associated Press State & Local Wire. 14 June 2003. Sports News.

155. "Hank Greenberg's heroics came on a dreary, rainy day." Green, Jerry. "Thrilling tiebreaker cracks Tigers' top five games." *Detroit News.* 8 October 2009.

155. "Greenberg wasn't sure if he was awake or dreaming." Habib, Hal. "When baseball went to war." *Palm Beach Post.* 23 March 2003. P. 1B.

CREDITS

NBLA/MLB PHOTOS: COVER (Foxx, Feller, Robinson, Gibson, Williams, DiMaggio, Patkin, Spahn); 8; 11; 12-13; 14-15; 16-17 (2); 19; 20; 24; 26; 28; 29; 31; 32; 37; 41; 44; 46; 47; 49; 50; 51; 52; 54; 56; 58-59; 60-61; 63; 64-65; 66-67; 68-69; 70; 72; 75; 77; 80; 82-83; 84-85 (Gibson); 85; 86; 88; 90-91; 93; 94-95; 96-97; 98; 101; 102; 105; 108-109; 110; 113; 114; 115; 116; 118-119; 120; 122-123; 126; 127; 136; 138-139; 140-141; 144; 146-147; 149; 150-151

UPI/CORBIS: 22-23

BURNS/GETTY IMAGES: 34-35

TRANSCENDENTAL GRAPHICS/GETTY IMAGES: 38-39; 134-135; 142-143

LOS ANGELES DODGERS/MLB PHOTOS: 42-43

AP PHOTO: 78-79; 130-131

WASHINGTON POST/GETTY IMAGES: 106

FROEBER/GETTY IMAGES: 125

REQUENA/MLB PHOTOS: 128

VANDIVERT/GETTY IMAGES: 133

HULTON ARCHIVE/GETTY IMAGES: 152-153

GRIFFIN/GETTY IMAGES: 154

INDEX

21 Club, 62
A League of Their Own, 57
A Winner Never Quits, 48
Aaron, Hank, 7
Abbott, Jim, 48
Academy Award, 148
Adams, Russell, 21
All-American Girls Professional Baseball League (AAGPBL), 7, 57
All-Star Game, 9, 10, 27, 48, 119, 141, 155
Allen, Ethan, 40
Allen, Mel, 119
Allied Forces, 55
Alomar, Roberto, 36
American Association, 121
American Baseball Bureau, 73
Amsterdam News, 74
Amyotrophic Lateral Sclerosis (ALS), 147
Appling, Luke, 25
Arizona Republic, 67
Ashburn, Richie, 87, 92
Atherton, Mo., 112
"Babe Ruth Day," 153
Baker, Del, 131
Baltimore Orioles, 9, 67
"Bambino," 153
Bankhead, Dan, 76, 81, 99
Banks, Ernie, 21, 50
Barber, Walter Lanier "Red," 119
Barrett, Charles "Red," 30, 33
Bartman, Steve, 111
Baseball Hall of Fame, 10, 13, 21, 27, 61, 62, 69, 81, 87, 92, 107, 109, 112, 134, 141, 145, 153
Baseball Hall of Fame Veterans Committee, 18, 21, 81, 141
"Baseball's Greatest Living Ballplayer," 9
Battle of the Bulge, 107, 155
Battle of the Philippines, 55
Bearden, Gene, 87, 99, 131
Beazley, Johnny, 87, 89, 99
Beazley, John Jr., 89
Bell, "Cool Papa," 81
Benton, Al, 155
Berg, Gus, 153
Berg, Morris "Moe," 55
Berle, Milton, 53
Bevens, Bill, 139
"Big Poison," 17
Billy Goat Tavern, 117
Birmingham Barons, 18
"Black Babe Ruth," 148
Black Sox scandal, 69
Blasingame, Don, 112
Bluege, Ossie, 107
Bostic, Joe, 74

Boston Braves, 13, 17, 18, 25, 30, 36, 62, 67, 72, 87, 89. 103, 119, 131, 145, 148
Boston Braves Historical Society, 18
Boston Globe, 122
Boston Red Sox, 13, 18, 21, 30, 40, 55, 73, 89, 99, 104, 112, 117, 122, 129, 131, 141
Boudreau, Lou, 36, 99, 117, 119, 131
Bowman, Bob, 122
"Boy Manager," 117
Bradley, Alva, 117
Branca, Ralph, 36, 74, 112, 139
Breadon, Sam, 69, 145
Brecheen, Harry, 141
Breen, Gerard, 40
Bremerton, Wash., 153
Breslin, Jimmy, 9
Brett, George, 10
Brissie, Lou, 48
Broeg, Bob, 122, 132, 134
Brooklyn Dodgers, 7, 18, 36, 43, 53, 57, 61, 62, 69, 71, 73, 74, 76, 81, 85, 87, 97, 99, 119, 122, 124, 129, 132, 134, 139, 141, 145, 153
Bronze Star, 53, 104
Brown, Willard, 76
Buckner, Bill, 139
Bull Durham, 111
Bush, George "Poppy," 35, 40
Cactus League, 67
Cairo, Ill., 144
Camilli, Dolph, 132
Camp Breckenridge, 57
Camp Custer, 53
Camp Edwards, 50
Campanella, Roy, 43, 61, 99
Cannon, Jimmy, 153
Cape Girardeau, Mo., 144
Carey, Max, 57
Caribbean World Series, 36
Carlson, Hal, 13
Carpenter, Ruly Jr., 119
Carter, Gary, 112
Carty, Rico, 36
Cascade Mountain Range, 153
Casey, Hugh, 33, 139, 141
Case, George, 36
Cashman, Joe, 122
Caster, George, 33
Castro, Fidel, 36
Chandler, Albert Benjamin "Happy," 69, 122, 124, 141
Chapman, Ben, 25, 97
Chicago Cubs, 30, 36, 48, 67, 92, 111, 137, 141, 155
Chicago Tribune, 117

Chicago White Sox, 9, 25, 69, 81, 111
Cincinnati Reds, 30, 33, 36, 47, 53, 69, 73, 112, 148
Clark, Allie, 131
Clarke, Fred, 107
Clary, Ellis, 48, 134
Cleveland Indians, 21, 53, 67, 81, 85, 92, 99, 100, 117, 119, 121, 131, 145
Cleveland Plain Dealer, 100
Cleveland Press, 67
"Clown Prince of Baseball," 53, 111
Cobb, Ty, 30, 134
Cochrane, Mickey, 28, 109
Cole, Mel, 155
College World Series, 35
Columbia Law School, 55
Comiskey Park, 25, 121
Congressional Medal of Honor, 53
Cooper, Gary, 148
Cooper, Mort, 89, 112, 145
Cooper, Walker, 112, 145
Cotton Club, 122
Cox, William, 119
Cramer, Richard Ben, 35, 107
Crosby, Bing, 155
Crosley Field, 7, 25
Culberson, Leon, 141
"Curse of the Bambino," 10, 117
"Curse of the Billy Goat," 111, 117
D-Day, 47, 155
Daley, Arthur, 73
Dandridge, Ray, 62
Danson, Ted, 145
Davis, Pepper Paire, 57
Day, Laraine, 122
Day, Leon, 62
Dean, Dizzy, 76, 121
Detroit Tigers, 10, 47, 81, 92, 97, 111, 117, 131, 137, 155
DeWitt, Bill, 134
DiMaggio, Dom, 18, 30, 137, 141
DiMaggio, Joe, 7, 9, 10, 35, 55, 107, 109, 111, 119, 122, 129, 137, 141, 145, 147
Disco Demolition Night, 121
Dobson, Joe, 131, 141
Doby, Larry, 62, 67, 71, 81, 85, 121
Doerr, Bobby, 18, 21, 89
Dorsey, Tommy, 33
"Double X," 13
Doubleday, Abner, 121
Dressen, Charlie, 74
Drysdale, Don, 43
"Ducky," 121
Durocher, Leo, 18, 69, 71, 122, 124, 132

Dykes, Jimmy, 30
"Dysart Deer," 145
Early, Joe, 67
Eastern League, 92, 111
Eastman, Joseph, 55
Ebbets Field, 43, 62, 71, 122, 132, 139
Edge, Bob, 141
Edwards, Bruce, 139
"Eephus" pitch, 27
Eig, Jonathan, 71
Eisenhower, Dwight, 104
Engelberg, Memphis, 122
Ennis, Del, 92, 97
Erskine, Carl, 74
ESPN, 40, 43
Federal Office of Defense Transportation, 55
Feller, Bob, 7, 25, 27, 35, 45, 53, 55, 67, 74, 99, 103, 131, 145
Feller, Marguerite, 25
Fenway Park, 27, 36, 43, 122
Ferrell, Rick, 112
Ferrell, Wes, 112
Flood, Curt, 121, 124
Flxible Clipper bus, 62
Forbes Field, 10
Fort Hood, Texas, 57
Fort Wayne Dixies, 57
Foxx, Jimmie, 13, 55, 57
Frazee, Harry, 117
French, Larry, 132
Gaedel, Eddie, 81, 121
Galehouse, Denny, 131, 145
Gallagher, Jim, 48, 50
Gardella, Danny, 124
"Gashouse Gang," 121
Gay, Timothy, 74
Gehrig, Eleanor, 147
Gehrig, Lou, 55, 147, 148
Gehringer, Charlie, 30, 55
Georgetown University, 73
Gibson, Josh, 27, 81, 147, 148, 153
Gibson, Truman, 57
Giebell, Floyd, 131
Gilbert, Charlie, 92
Gillette, 141
Gionfriddo, Al, 137, 139, 145
Glendale, Ariz., 43
Gonzalez, Mike, 141
"Good Old Joe Early Night," 67
Gordon, Joe, 21, 55, 67, 89, 141
Gordon, Sid, 97
Goslin, Goose, 28
"Grandma," 33
Grand Rapids Chicks, 57
Gray, Pete, 7, 47, 48
Great Depression, 28

Great Lakes Naval Training Center, 109
"Green Light Letter," 45
Greenberg, Hank, 10, 30, 45, 53, 137, 155
"Greenberg Gardens," 10
Greene County, Mo., 141
Griffith, Clark, 45
Griffith Park, 104
Grim, Bob, 99
Grimm, Charlie, 27, 121
Grossman, Harry, 50
Grove, Lefty, 7, 13, 25, 30
Gutteridge, Don, 134
Gwynn, Tony, 10
Haines, Jesse, 69
"Hammerin' Hank," 10
Harder, Mel, 13
Harris, Bucky, 119
Hartje, Chris, 155
Hartung, Clint, 112
Hatten, Joe, 132
Havana, Cuba, 122
Heinz, W.C., 33
Heisenberg, Werner, 55
Henrich, Tommy, 121, 139
Herman, Babe, 112
Hershberger, Willard, 147, 148
Hodges, Russ, 99
"Hog Jaws," 112
Holman, Bud, 43
Holman Stadium, 43
Holmes, Tommy, 17, 18, 145
Homestead Grays, 21, 27, 153
"Hondo Hurricane," 112
Hope, Bob, 155
Howard, Elston, 21
Hubbell, Carl, 13
Hutchings, Johnny, 13
Hyames Field, 40
International League, 74
"Iron Horse," 147, 148
Japanese Baseball Hall of Fame, 55
Jensen, Jackie, 40
Jersey City Giants, 74
Immerman, Connie, 122
Information Please!, 55
International League, 145
Irvine, Monte, 62, 74
Jackie Robinson Award, 73
Jackie Robinson Day, 71
Jackson, "Shoeless Joe," 69
Jakuchi, Sig, 134
James, Bob, 155
Jansen, Larry, 73, 97
Japanese Imperial Navy, 55
Joe DiMaggio: The Hero's Life, 35, 107

159

Johnson, Richard, 117
Johnson, "Sweet Lou," 21
Johnson, Walter, 103, 112
"Joltin' Joe," 121, 145
Jones, David, 109
Joost, Eddie, 17, 148
Jorgensen, Spider, 139
Journal Square, 74
Kaese, Harold, 122
Kageura, Masaru, 55
Kalamazoo, Mich., 35, 40
Kaline, Al, 30
Kansas City Monarchs, 21, 33, 57, 76, 85
Keeler, Willie, 9
Kell, George, 30
Keller, Charlie, 141
Keltner, Ken, 10, 131
Kenosha Comets, 57
Kinder, Ellis, 129, 131
Kiner, Ralph, 10
"Kiner's Korner," 13
Kinnaman, Bob, 155
Klinger, Bob, 141
Kluszewski, Ted, 36
"Knights of the Keyboard," 122
Koufax, Sandy, 43
Kramer, Jack, 18, 131, 145
Laabs, Chet, 134
La Guardia, Fiorello, 147, 148
Landis-Eastman Line, 55
Landis, Kenesaw "Mountain," 44, 45, 55, 61, 69, 119
Lanier, Max, 124, 145
Lavagetto, Cookie, 137, 139
Lemmon, Jack, 145
Lemon, Bob, 99
Leonard, Buck, 21
Life magazine, 139
Life of Christ, 71
Lincoln, Abraham, 71
Lincoln Park, 7
Lincoln Tavern, 117
Little League World Series, 35, 40, 43
Lock Haven All-Stars, 40
Lohrke, Jack "Lucky," 155
Loidl, Ladislaus, 104
Lombardi, Ernie, 148
Lopez, Al, 87
Los Angeles Times, 124
"Losing Pitcher," 50
"Lou Gehrig Appreciation Day," 148
Louisville Colonels, 107
Ludendorff Bridge, 103
Lundy Lumber, 40
Lycoming Dairy, 40
Lyden, George, 155
Mack, Ray, 25
Macon, Max, 132
MacPhail, Larry, 124
Maglie, Sal, 124
Malaney, Jack, 122
Manley, Abe, 62
Manley, Effa, 62, 81
Mantle, Mickey, 121
Marcus Hook, Pa., 104
Marion, Marty, 89, 145
Maris, Roger, 121
Marshall, Willard, 97
Martinez, Fred, 155
Masi, Phil, 145
"Master Melvin," 13
Maynard Midgets, 40
Mayo Clinic, 147
Mays, Willie, 18, 21
Mathewson, Christy, 30
McCarthy, Joe, 131, 147, 148
McKechnie, Bill, 47, 148
McLemore, Henry, 141
McNally, Dave, 124
McQuinn, George, 155

Medwick, Joe, 121, 122, 132
Melton, Cliff, 99
Memphis Chicks, 47
Memphis Red Sox, 76
Metkovich, George, 107
Mexican League, 81, 124
Meyerhoff, Art, 57
Mr. Coffee, 9
Michigan Avenue, 117
Miksis, Eddie, 139
Milwaukee Brewers, 121
Milwaukee Chicks, 57
Minneapolis Millerettes, 57
Minoso, Minnie, 121
Mize, Johnny, 13, 61, 137
Monroe, Marilyn, 9
Montague Street, 71
Montreal Royals, 36, 74
Monument Park, 148
Moore, Donnie, 139
Moore, Jerry, 17
Moore, Terry, 145
Morales, Pablo, 36
Most Valuable Player Award, 7, 9, 10, 18, 21, 25, 30, 40, 89, 119, 122, 129
Mota, Manny, 36, 43
Mueller, Don, 112
Mulcahy, Hugh, 50, 53
Municipal Stadium, 67, 100
"Murderers' Row," 148
Murphy, Johnny, 33
"Muscles," 121
Musial, Stan, 7, 25, 47, 55, 61, 74, 87, 132, 134, 145
Mutual Broadcasting System, 141
My Turn at Bat, 122
NAACP, 62
NBC-TV, 141
Negro Leagues, 7, 18, 21, 33, 57, 61, 62, 71, 74, 76, 85, 100, 153
Newcombe, Don, 99, 100
Newsday, 121
New York Giants, 13, 21, 25, 53, 61, 67, 73, 74, 97, 99, 112, 124, 132, 155
New York Mets, 13
New York Post, 153
New York Times, The, 53, 73, 87, 112, 147
New York Yankees, 21, 35, 53, 61, 62, 67, 87, 89, 97, 100, 107, 117, 119, 122, 129, 134, 139, 141, 145, 147
New Yorker Hotel, 122
Newark Eagles, 62, 81
Newhouser, Hal, 7, 25, 28
Newsom, Bobo, 124, 131
Nippon Professional Baseball League, 55
"No No Nanette," 117
Nuxhall, Joe, 7, 25, 47
Nuxhall, Orville, 47
O'Neil, Buck, 21, 74, 76
Oakland Oaks, 21
Office of Strategic Services, 55
"Old Perfessor," 61
"Old Reliable," 121
Opening Day, 71
Ortiz, David, 36
Osaka Tigers, 55
Ostermueller, Fritz, 76
Ott, Mel, 7, 13, 97
Owen, Mickey, 124, 137, 139
Pacific Coast League, 21
Page, Joe, 33, 132
Paige, Satchel, 21, 25, 27, 33, 74, 76, 81, 85, 100, 153
Palmer, Jim, 40
Paoli, Pa., 111
Papini, Giovanni, 71
Parks, Rosa, 57
Parnell, Mel, 89, 129, 131

Patkin, Max, 67, 111
Paterson, Bob, 155
Patterson, Robert, 107
Paul, Gabe, 148
Pearl Harbor, Hawaii, 7, 27, 30, 45, 48, 53, 103
Peckinpaugh, Roger, 117
Pellagrini, Eddie, 89
Pesky, Johnny, 18, 89, 92, 137, 141
Philadelphia Athletics, 10, 13, 48, 155
Philadelphia Phillies, 50, 81, 92, 97, 119
Piazza, Mike, 45
Picetti, Vic, 155
Pipp, Wally, 147
Pittsburgh Crawfords, 27, 153
Pittsburgh Pirates, 10, 17, 27, 62, 124
Polner, Murray, 69
Polo Grounds, 13, 53, 99, 112
Posey, Cumberland, 153
Potomac Line, 55
Potter, Nels, 134, 155
Price, Jackie, 67
Prieto, Oscar, 36
Princeton University, 55
"Prince Hal," 30
Purple Heart, 53, 104
"Putt-Putt," 92
Pyongyang, Korea, 109
Quinn, Frank, 129
Racine Belles, 57
Raft, George, 122
"Rapid Robert," 7, 25
Raschi, Vic, 129
Reader's Digest, 76
Reardon, John "Beans," 17
Reese, Pee Wee, 103
Reiser, Pete, 18, 73, 132
Remagen, Germany, 103
Rice, Grantland, 48
Rice, Jim, 21
Rickey, Branch, 7, 61, 69, 71, 73, 74, 76, 87, 112, 119, 153
Riddle, Elmer, 112
Riddle, Johnny, 112
Risk, George, 155
Rizzuto, Phil, 74, 89, 121, 122, 129, 137
Roberts, Robin, 92, 97
Robinson, Jackie, 7, 36, 45, 57, 69, 71, 73, 74, 76, 81, 85, 87, 97, 99, 119, 122, 153
Rockford Peaches, 7, 57
Rookie of the Year Award, 73, 87, 97, 100
Roosevelt, Franklin D., 44, 45, 147
Roosevelt, Theodore, 69
Roosevelt Stadium, 74
Rose, Pete, 17
Rose Bowl, 40
Rosenthal, Larry, 25
Rowe, Schoolboy, 131
Rubenstein, Helena, 57
Ruppert Stadium, 62
Ruth, Babe, 13, 35, 55, 73, 112, 117, 147, 153
Ryan, Nolan, 40
Ryukyu Islands, 55
St. Louis Browns, 7, 18, 47, 76, 100, 121, 134, 137, 144, 145, 155
St. Louis Cardinals, 36, 47, 61, 69, 87, 89, 119, 121, 122, 124, 129, 132, 134, 144, 145
St. Louis Post-Dispatch, 122, 132
Sain, Johnny, 74, 145
Salvation Army, 109
Satchel: The Life and Times of an American Legend, 27
Sawamura, Eiji, 55
Schacht, Al, 53
Schmidt, Mike, 40

Schumacher, Garry, 112
"Scooter," 121
Seaver, Tom, 40
Selective Service Act, 50
Serie del Caribe, 36
Sewell, Luke, 134
Sewell, Rip, 27
Shea, Spec, 139
Shibe Park, 10, 13, 97
Shea Stadium, 45
Shepard, Bert, 104
Shirley, "Tex," 134
Shor, "Toots," 35
"Shot Heard 'Round the World," 74, 99, 112
Shotton, Burt, 139, 145
Sianis, Bill, 111, 117
"Silent Captain of the Red Sox," 21
Slater, Bill, 141
Slaughter, Enos, 7, 18, 137, 141, 144, 145
Slim Sallee, 33
Smith, Ed, 9
Smith, Hilton, 33, 74
Smith, Red, 18
"Smokes for Servicemen," 53
Snoqualmie Pass highway, 155
South Bend Blue Sox, 57
Southern Association, 107
Southern League, 47
Southworth, Billy, 89
"Sow Belly," 112
Spahn, Warren, 25, 103, 104
Spink, J.G. Taylor, 100
"Splendid Splinter," 10, 28
Spokane Indians, 153
Sporting News, 53, 100
Sportsman's Park, 145, 155
Stan Musial: An American Life, 87
"Stan the Man," 132
Stanky, Eddie, 139
Stanton, Bob, 141
"Staten Island Scot," 99
Stengel, Casey, 17, 55, 61, 62, 67, 103, 121, 129
Stephens, Vern, 18, 134
Stewart, Bill, 145
Stoneham, Horace, 13, 67
Stout, Glenn, 117
Stotz, Carl, 35, 40, 43
"Streetcar Series," 145
Sukeforth, Clyde, 71, 73, 74
Sundra, Steve, 134
Tebbetts, Birdie, 129
"Teddy Ballgame," 9
"The Beast," 13
"The Birmingham Gentleman," 21
The Catcher Was a Spy, 55
"The Gentleman First Baseman," 104
"The Lip," 122
The Pride of the Yankees, 148
Thomson, Bobby, 74, 97, 99, 112
Thompson, Hank, 76
Time magazine, 124
Topping, Dan, 35, 62
Travis, Cecil, 107
Triple Crown, 21, 121, 122
Trucks, Virgil, 137
Tunney, Gene, 53
Tye, Larry, 27
UCLA, 57
Ueberroth, Peter, 50
Ulithi Atoll, 104
University of California, 35, 40
University of Illinois, 117
University of Michigan, 92
United States Armed Forces, 50
United States Army, 48, 103, 107
U.S. District Court, 124
United States Marines, 109
United States Navy, 97, 104, 137, 155
USS Alabama, 53
USS Helena, 99

Utica Blue Sox, 92
Vaughan, Bob, 124
Vaughan, Glenn, 123
Vaughan, Joseph Floyd "Arky," 124
Vecsey, George, 87
Veeck, Bill, 61, 67, 71, 81, 100, 121
Veeck As In Wreck, 67, 81
Veracruz Azules, 124
Vernon, Mickey, 104
Vero Beach, Fla., 43
Voiselle, Bill, 99
Wakefield, Dick, 27, 87, 92, 97
Walker, Harry, 92, 141
Wall Street Journal, 21
Walter Reed Hospital, 104
Walters, Bucky, 112
Waner, Lloyd, 17
Waner, Paul, 17
War Department, 48
Ward, Leo, 132
Washington Motor Coach, 153
Washington Senators, 104, 107, 139
"Waste Fat Night," 53
Webb, Del, 35, 62
Webb, Mel, 122
Weiss, George, 62
Wells, Willie, 62, 85
West Madison Street, 117
Westcott, Rich, 119
Western Michigan University, 40
"Whitey" Ashburn, 92
Whitman, Burt, 122
Whiz Kids, 92
Whyatt, Whit, 132
Williams, Billy, 50
Williams, May, 109
Williams, Ted, 7, 9, 10, 18, 21, 28, 36, 40, 55, 89, 92, 107, 109, 122, 129
Williamsport, Pa., 35, 40, 43
Wilson, Artie, 21
Wilson, Hack, 13
Wilson Junior High School, 47
World Series, 7, 33, 36, 67, 69, 99, 100, 117, 119, 129, 131, 134, 137, 139, 141, 145
World War II, 7, 18, 21, 25, 30, 33, 43, 45, 47, 48, 53, 55, 57, 74, 81, 99, 103, 107, 109, 117, 134, 144, 153, 155
Wright, Taft, 25
Wrigley, Philip K., 48, 50, 57, 117
Wrigley Field, 43, 48, 50, 111
Van Robays, Maurice, 27
Yale University, 35, 40, 119
Yawkey, Tom, 18, 30
"Yankee Clipper," 9, 35, 107, 111, 145
Yankee Stadium, 145, 148, 153
Yastrzemski, Carl, 21
Yomiuri Giants, 55
York, Rudy, 131
Young, Cy, 30, 103